I KNOW WE'RE ALL WELCOME AT THE TABLE

Much has been written about the political divide in this country and our need to find ways of getting along with those who have ideas and perspectives that are radically different from ours. Janice Springer has given us a perfect opportunity to finally tell the truth and find our way. The title grabs us and invites us inside where Janice outlines the tools we need to make peace happen -- and it's not as hard as you might think. These tools come straight out of her Christian ministry but they apply to all of us of any faith tradition. Janice uses her own journey to demystify the work we all must do. Her honesty and openness give us hope that we can also succeed to find compassion over judgment and transform ourselves and our community. She not only shows us the tools, she shows us how to be gentle with ourselves as we practice and how to share these tools with others in our communities. We CAN become the change we want to see thanks to Janice Springer.

– Betsy Mulligan-Dague
Executive Director, Jeannette Rankin Peace Center
Missoula, MT

The eye-catching title of this intriguing book is a gracious invitation to honestly embrace the reality of plurality in our lives when considering relationships and diverse angles of vision on controversial issues. The simple, yet poignant message regarding human relationships is encapsulated in the theme of this work to: "Bless them - Change me!" It is inevitable that we will come into contact with people with whom we differ in thought, word or deed; hence conflict is inescapable. The author judiciously proposes ideas and activities that create the possibility for transformation of our attitudes and actions. She draws from diverse religious traditions to illustrate her concerns by providing inspirational quotations followed by penetrating questions to clearly and cogently impact her audience.

Her refreshingly personal, honest, and humble authenticity and transparency is evident throughout the book and lends credibility to what she writes. She candidly uses narratives from her own experiences and identifies the barriers created by prejudicial postures that knowingly or unknowingly result in human division. The centrality of relationships, the necessity of community, the power of forgiveness and acceptance are precursors to the inner transformation that leads to loving and accepting relationships. This book can be utilized in diverse settings and is immeasurably helpful for individuals and communities in creating accepting and loving relationships.

– Robert H. Albers, PhD
Distinguished Visiting Professor of Pastoral Theology (retired)
United Theological Seminary of the Twin Cities

In her inspiring book, Janice Springer helps us understand and live by this testing prayer: "O God, bless them. Change me." This remarkable and transformative book provides ample hands-on activities and prayers on how to love in action and how to live respectfully with our "enemies" from the same faith or different faiths without feeling threatened by them.

This book is an essential reading for intrafaith and interfaith peacemaking and community building. Though it is written from the perspective of a devout Christian, it could be modified to other faiths as well, as long as the participants are willing to listen patiently, and cherish the others' stories.

– Dema Kazkaz
President
Masjid Al Noor Islamic Center, Waterloo, Iowa

I KNOW WE'RE ALL WELCOME AT THE TABLE, BUT DO I HAVE TO SIT NEXT TO YOU?

To my cousins Lee and Norma, with love —

Janice Jean Springer

JANICE JEAN SPRINGER

Energion Publications
Gonzalez, FL
2018

eBook Editions:
Aer.io: 978-1-63199-536-1
Kindle: 978-1-63199-537-8
iBooks: 978-1-63199-538-5
Google: 978-1-63199-539-2

Author photo (back cover) by Christie Goodman.

Print Edition
ISBN10: 1-63199-534-0
ISBN13: 978-1-63199-534-7
Library of Congress Control Number: 2018947688

Energion Publications
P. O. Box 841
Gonzalez, FL 32560
850-525-3916

energion.com
pubs@energion.com

DEDICATION

Joshua, Lucia, Jessica and Ella,
my amazing, beautiful, talented, crazy grandchildren,
I love you!
You are the reason I do this work,
and so, I dedicate this book to you.

May you and all our children live in peace
and know the power of love.

TABLE OF CONTENTS

Part 3: Inviting Others to Join Us at the Welcome Table

A Leader's Guide:

PART 1:
SETTING THE
WELCOME TABLE

FOREWORD

By chance in late 2016 I met the Reverend Janice Jean Springer. In a weekly newsletter e-mail I saw there was an upcoming all-day workshop titled *I Know We're All Welcome at the Table, But Do I Have to Sit Next To You?* The catchy title made me laugh but also left me wondering what was this about? After reading the initial description of the workshop I had a feeling this was more than a sappy session on how it's important to try and get along with everybody. Most people know it's better to have peace and harmony than conflict and disorder, but how do you begin to make this happen? I wanted to believe this workshop could be a guiding light on how a person could begin the messy yet rewarding journey of truly striving to love everyone.

Seeing as this workshop was only an hour south from where I lived I decided to go see it for myself. After listening to Janice and her message I left with a new outlook on the world's problems. My spirit had been uplifted and yet humbled. I realized if I wanted to do my part to change the world, the first thing I would need to do is change myself.

I felt strongly about what I heard so I invited Janice to come up to my church in the small town of Osage, Iowa so she could lead her workshop. We had a group made up of both church members, friends from the community, and some who even traveled over two hours from Minneapolis. By the time we were done several people told me how great this workshop was and how they hoped Janice would come back again for to do a different workshop—which she did. (Even now as I write this members of my church have been asking me, "When will Janice be coming back to do another workshop?")

When I learned Janice was writing a book based on her workshop I was thrilled, because I believe the words you—the reader—are about to read have the power to change your life.

You will find in this book a mantra repeated again and again, saying, "O God, bless them, change me." When we encounter someone who disagrees with us on religion, politics, or any of our treasured beliefs our first instinct oftentimes is to dig our heels into the ground and say we're the ones in the right and the other person needs to change their thinking—and until they do we're either going to blatantly ignore them or brazenly point out all the reasons why they're wrong.

As you read through the pages of this book you will be invited on a rewarding yet at times an uneasy journey. You will be invited to look beyond your own perspective and to try and perceive issues through the eyes of your enemies. You will be invited to consider that instead of working hard to make your enemies change you need to first listen to their stories, feel their pain, and try to understand why they believe what they believe. In the New Testament we see the words of Jesus where he says, "...Love your enemies and pray for those who persecute you, so that you may be children of your Father in heaven..." (Matthew 5:44-45 NRSV). Out of all the teachings of Jesus this one has to be the most challenging. The words in this book can teach us how to love and pray for our enemies.

This book could not be published at a more needed time. The society around us has grown too hostile—especially our politics. Instead of living in a society that values respectful dialogue and compromise we've entrenched ourselves in an "us versus them" mentality. How are we to stop this constant anger? While we cannot control the attitudes of the people around us, the most powerful gift we can give is to strive to live each day modeling the peace we want for the world.

As I already said once and I'll say it again: the words in this book will make you feel uneasy. Yet these words will also fill your spirit with hope, life, and new positive energy. This book can help you to be in meaningful relationship with those difficult people you struggle to love. Blessings to you as you begin this journey.

The Rev. Charles D. Owens
Pastor of Osage United Church of Christ
Osage, Iowa
2018

SAYING GRACE AT THE TABLE:
OFFERING THANKS

I like to imagine a very big table where many people are gathered, a welcome table where all the diverse gifts come together to make this book. As a gesture of respect and gratitude, I bow my head and give thanks.

Some of the people at that table read parts of the manuscript, giving me important feedback: Whitney Brown, Cheryl Cornish, Debbie Eisenbise, Christie Goodman, Karen Sanborn, Susan Weier, and Brewster Willcox. I thank each of you for your helpful suggestions and your enthusiastic support.

I am grateful to have Ken Arthur and David Moffett-Moore seated with us. You introduced me to Energion Publications. Henry and Jody Neufield, owners of Energion, are seated at the welcome table, too. You accepted this work for publication, for which I thank you both. I am grateful for your warmth, your personal attention, and your commitment to publishing important books. Chris Eyre was my editor. Chris, I thank you for your openness to my ideas and your patience when I questioned yours. I appreciate your pressing me to make space for some important additions.

Charles Owens is here at the table, sitting with Kate McDonough. I was energized by the interest that the two of you showed in my book. Your enthusiasm when we were at dinner one evening renewed my flagging spirit. And Charles, you called me one morning offering resources that I had given up finding, and suddenly I felt I was not alone. For that, I am very grateful.

Christie Goodman, we have a place at the welcome table for you. More times than I can count, my conversations with you began, "I have a little computer question. Do you have a minute?" You knew that *little* and *minute* were grossly incorrect descriptions of what would be required for you to rescue the manuscript from my computer ignorance. Thanks for being always generous with your time and energy and—bless you!—always patient with me.

When I needed people and places who were willing to support and promote this work, several people offered suggestions and made contacts for me. Most of those folks are already seated at our welcome table…Whitney, Cheryl, Debbie, Brewster, Susan, Charles…but I want to set a place for Rita Waggoner, too. Thanks, Rita, for your suggestions of people who might serve as resources and especially for your conviction that I should keep writing.

Richard Schuster, you didn't expect to be invited to the table. You've probably forgotten, but I haven't: you were the one who asked me to help the regional body of your church denomination hold together in spite of their great differences, and that was the birth of *I Know We're All Welcome at the Table, But Do I Have to Sit Next to You?* Thank you for inviting me to begin the journey that resulted in this book.

I don't know how we'll get them all around our table, but these need to be here, too: the participants—over 350 of you so far—in the many workshops on this material that I have led. Your responses convinced me that writing this book was important.

I am grateful for that, and for all I learned from you.

Susan Weier sits right next to me at the table. I thank you, Susan, for your support, encouragement and love….30 years and still counting.

And of course, present at this table with us, always with us: the Holy One, whose inspiration is the source of this work. For all I have named, and any I have forgotten, for the gifts and graces given so generously, I give great thanks.

INTRODUCTION

The phone call came from a regional body of the United Church of Christ in a major metropolitan area. The churches that made up this association were so diverse that they found it not only difficult to relate to one another; they were now experiencing open conflict. Though of the same denomination, they had great diversity in race, economics, ethnic background, theology and even language.

They had heard that I led workshops and retreats. Would I come to a meeting of their association and offer some kind of program that would help them get along with one another, something that might offer them some tools for relating amidst such challenging differences?

Well, yes, I did lead workshops. (Well, I'd led one or two.) I was sure I could offer them something that would help. (I hadn't the slightest idea what that could be.) Yes, I would come. (Fools rush in where angels fear to tread.)

That was the beginning of my journey with *I Know We're All Welcome at the Table, But Do I Have to Sit Next to You?* I created a workshop with that title and offered it to the one hundred or so people who came that day. It went well, and participants were very enthusiastic. Some wanted to hold similar workshops in their own churches, and asked for my help. Over the next several years, I offered this workshop many times in many places. It always generated enthusiasm and appreciation. I began to think about putting this material into a book.

At first, I wondered if this material is still relevant. By the time I began to consider writing a book, years had passed since that original workshop. Was there still a need to keep offering peace-making tools? Then I listened to the evening news.

There are terrorist attacks around the world and mass shootings in the USA. Schools hold lock-down drills. Hostility and accusations define the presidential campaign. Hate crimes increase. Graphic violence is the most popular form of entertainment. Racism leads to accusations of police brutality. Muslims become the enemy of choice. The practice of civility seems not to be valued.

Yes. There is a need for this book.

In writing a book, I had several questions to consider. Do I want to speak only to the Christian community, or would this material be appropriate for people of other faiths, or no religious faith? I live and serve within the Christian tradition, but my interfaith perspective makes this book accessible and useful to all people, regardless of the tradition in which they stand or the spirituality that they practice. I bring the insights of other paths to my own spiritual practice, and I bring them to this writing.

I understand that some people do not find traditional names for Ultimate Reality useful. While I am comfortable using the name God, I also address God in other ways, such as Holy One, Sacred Mystery, Ground of Being, Spirit, Source, Creator, Beloved. Blessed be God's holy names.

I am drawn to those teachings that we find in all the wisdom traditions—the major world religions—of our species. All our spiritual traditions speak of forgiveness. They all demand justice. They all advocate peace. They all call us to a life of service. Despite our different faiths, we can work together to make this earth a healed and healing home. This book offers a small effort to that end.

I faced another challenge when I decided to turn the workshop into a book. When I lead a workshop, I am, at least for a few hours, in relationship with the participants. I can read their body language, hear their questions or concerns. I can tell when I am losing them, and make immediate adjustments. But when this material is in the form of a book, I have no relationship with readers like you. I can't tell if you are still with me. I don't know your questions and can't respond to your concerns. My words are in print, final, no in-the-moment adjustments possible. I can't do a lot about that, but I can encourage you to read this book in company with a book club or one other person so you have a place to reflect and process the ideas here. You are also welcome to contact me.

I hope this book will be helpful to you as you try to live respectfully with those who are different from yourself. In the Leaders' Guide, I have given you the tools you need to share this information with others. I have designed this material so it is easy to understand and easy to remember (though not always easy to do!) The tone is non-judgmental and empowering.

I know we are all welcome at the table, and I want to sit next to you. I hope this book will help all of us find our way into love.

Part 2:
Feasting at the
Welcome Table

CHAPTER 1: TELLING THE TRUTH ABOUT OUR LIVES

I don't want to talk to them,
I can't get along with them,
I am against them, and they're against me.
Their opinions make me sore,
What they stand for I deplore,
I just want to turn away and go out the door![1]

I pride myself on being a person of radical welcome. I sing *Let There Be Peace on Earth* with the best of them. I can recite those gospel verses about loving your enemies. But…if I'm going to tell the truth about my life, this old song is closer to my reality.

I have no more time for them,
I can't stand the sight of them,
I am against them and they're against me.
We are different to the core.
All their problems I'll ignore!
I just want to turn away and go out the door![2]

What happens between *Let There Be Peace on Earth* and "I can't stand the sight of them?" How do I move so easily from here to there? Why is it so hard to live what I profess?

In this book, I'm going to offer some simple tools that can enable us to welcome those we'd rather not welcome, tools that can help us to stay in community with the people who drive us crazy. These tools are simple…but not easy. They will challenge our ego's

---

1   Avery, Richard. and Donald Marsh. "In the Presence of My Enemies."
     The Second Avery and Marsh Songbook. (agape. Carol Stream, IL, 1983),
     17-18.

2   Ibid.

craving to be right, to be superior, to be in control. That challenge is a central task of the faith journey, and it is a task we prefer to avoid.

FAITH AS INNER TRANSFORMATION

Before we return to our shift from *Let There Be Peace on Earth* to "I can't stand the sight of them," consider the relationship between the ego and a decision to be a people of peace and compassion. The ego is the part of us that describes and defends. Perhaps my ego describes me as a good preacher who is faithful to the right religion. But life is constantly challenging those descriptive words *good, faithful, right,* and so my ego must defend me. It is my ego doing its job when I am angry. My ego has convinced me that I am my descriptions, and so my very being depends on this internal, barely conscious process of describing and defending.

All of our great faith traditions address this problem. Our world religions teach us that we are not our descriptions, but something much deeper, and we don't need to defend those descriptions. They all teach us how to have something besides ego in the driver's seat. If we are Buddhist, we might talk about having the Buddha nature. Muslims emphasize surrender; the word Islam means surrender, or more fully, "the peace that comes when one's life is surrendered to God."[3] Christians talk about the indwelling Christ, or, as the apostle Paul said, "It is no longer I who live, but it is Christ who lives in me." [4]

The faith journey is about this inner transformation, and it is this inner transformation that makes it possible for us to love and forgive and respect. This work is not easy. Jean Vanier, founder of the international l'Arche communities where able-bodied and disabled people live together, writes, "The journey with Jesus is going to be a journey of transformation. We don't follow Jesus to

---

3   Smith, Huston. *Islam, A Concise Introduction*. (New York: Harper Collins, 2001), 2.
4   Galatians 2:20.

be comfortable."[5] As we explore ways to stay in community with people we wish would disappear, we will be doing not only the hard outer work of peacemaking, but also the hard inner work of transformation.

MOVING FROM WELCOME TO HOSTILITY

Now let's see how we make the shift from welcoming someone to naming him or her as enemy. I've been observing myself, and I can show you how it seems to happen for me. It might happen anywhere, in my family, with my co-workers, or in my neighborhood, but let me just use as an example a group that gathers every week for meditation or prayer.

In the abstract, I love all the people in my meditation group. We're all sacred beings, right? But then you and I differ on whether or not we should include some chanting with our meditation. I feel a little irritated with you.

Your culture—that might be race, ethnic background, sexual orientation, education, economic class—is different than mine. I don't want that to matter, but it does. I don't understand you or your way of looking at the world. I begin to feel uncomfortable around you.

In a discussion about the war, I learn that you support what I oppose. I discover that I'm becoming wary of you.

At our monthly potluck, we begin talking about immigration issues, and you and I are defending opposite positions. I'm starting not to like you very much.

I hear where you stand on gay marriage, and I stereotype you.

Another person makes a negative comment about you, and I add it to my arsenal, an arsenal I didn't even realize I was accumulating.

I start to avoid you, and to hang out with others who don't approve of you, either.

---

5   Vanier, Jean. Encountering the Other. (Mahuh, NJ: Paulist Press, 2006), 51.

We discuss a racial incident that happened in our town, and your ideas are so different from my own that I name you as one who is unfaithful. I now feel superior to you. What has happened, perhaps below my consciousness, is that you have become a threat to my deepest values and convictions. You have become my enemy and I must do something about that.

Now, I know how to be nice, so I'll be polite when we meet in our prayer group or at the grocery store. But don't let it fool you. In my mind, I have reduced you from a complex human being, full of mystery and contradictions and grace, to someone simple enough to fit into a box with a label. I have diminished you, and to diminish a person is to practice a kind of violence. In my mind, I have denied that you are one who hurts and hopes just like I do, one who is following the light as best she can, as I am. In my mind, you have become an "other," and I feel threatened. The Upanishads, sacred scripture in the Hindu tradition, state the situation clearly: *wherever there is other, there is fear.*[6] At a subtle level, my agenda will be to conquer you.

It is very humbling to acknowledge this progression in myself. Equally disturbing is recognizing that I probably won't even be judged for doing that to you, as long as I'm not outwardly nasty. Nearly any group of which I'm a part will give me permission to hate some kinds of people. The artistic circle I move in will jump all over me if I slur Jews, but they will make no comment if I trash Christians. My lesbian friends will protest insults to women or gays, but if I insult straight men, they will just laugh. In my own faith tradition, the church gives me permission (unconsciously) to diminish certain groups, even while we sing "They'll Know We are Christians By Our Love." A progressive church will give me permission to dismiss those who read the Bible literally. A conservative community will not say anything if I trash pro-choice folks. At my neighborhood barbeque, someone will call me on it if I speak negatively about African-Americans, but offer no opposition if I

---

6   Easwaran, Eknath. translator. *The Upanishads*. (Tomales, CA: Nilgiri Press, 1987) 144. Taittiriya Upanishad, part 11, section 7.

degrade Muslims. The circles I'm in give me permission to treat certain people as less worthy than me and my kind.

LOVE IS COMMANDED

But the world's sacred scriptures do not give me permission to diminish anyone. Pastor and author Eugene Peterson writes that the most distinctive thing about Christian love is that it is commanded.[7]

> *"You have heard that it was said, 'You shall love*
> *your neighbor and hate your enemy.' But I say*
> *to you, love your enemies and pray for those who*
> *persecute you."*[8]

Peterson reminds us that in the Christian gospels, love is a very big word. But it is not a valentine word.[9] Buddha would agree. The Dhammapada, a Buddhist scripture, quotes Buddha as saying "For hatred can never put an end to hatred. Love alone can."[10]

The 19th century Russian author Leo Tolstoy, an Orthodox Christian, wrote a story called "Resurrection". It tells of some soldiers, revolutionists and freedom fighters who are willing to give their lives to liberate the poor, the peasants, and the oppressed. One day they are captured, and they find themselves in a railroad car confined with many other prisoners: the poor, the peasants, and the oppressed. In those close quarters, the freedom fighters hate and despise the very ones for whom they were willing to die.

It's always easy to love in the abstract. It's always easy to be a peacemaker towards people you will never meet. But loving one another at the Thanksgiving family reunion or through community meetings or across the breakfast table...well, it is so much easier to

---

7 Peterson, Eugene H. *Christ Plays in Ten Thousand Places*. (Grand Rapids, MI: Wm. B. Eardmans Publishing Co., 2005), 326.
8 Matthew 5:43-44
9 Peterson. *Christ Plays in Ten Thousand Places*, 261.
10 Easwaran. Eknath, translator. *The Dhammapada*. (Tomales, CA: Nilgiri Press. 1985) 78. 1: Twin Verses. verses 5,6.

gather up our abstract commitment to love and take it somewhere else in search of people more lovable. I believe we are all welcome at the table -- whether that's the dinner table, the community potluck, or the Eucharist —but, really, do I have to sit next to you?

I suspect that some of us would not use a strong word like enemy when talking about relatives, neighbors or others in our faith community. But I'm going to hold us to that word. Simply because it is startling, a little offensive, even, it gets our attention. It helps us to look at something we might otherwise overlook. That's important, because until we recognize what we do to each other, we won't be able to do something else instead. It might also be helpful to remember the Aramaic word that we translate as enemy can also be translated as "someone with whom we are out of step."[11]

Jean Vanier, whom I quoted earlier, is my mentor on the subject of communities. He addresses our subject.

> *"There are many groups of people and many types of issue-oriented groups: against nuclear disarmament, against racism, for this or that. There is a danger, in issue-oriented groups not based on community, that the enemy is seen as being the one outside the group. The world gets divided between the good and the bad. We are among the good; the others are the bad. In issue-oriented groups, the enemy is always outside. We must struggle against all those who are outside of our group, all those who are of the other party. True community is different because of the realization that the evil is inside—not just inside the community, but inside me."[12]*

That old song with which I started this chapter continues with these words: "O my Lord, you set a table before me in the presence of my enemies."[13] A table is set for me, but it is never a private party. You are invited to that table, too, and so are all the people I don't want to be there. Over and over each day, I am challenged to

---

11   Vennard, Jane E. *Embracing the World: Praying for Justice and Peace.* (San Francisco: Jossey-Bass, 2002), 22, quoting Neil Douglas-Klotz.
12   Vanier, Jean. *From Brokenness to Community.* (Mahwah, NJ: Paulist Press, 1992), 49-50.
13   Avery and Marsh. "In the Presence of My Enemies".

love more deeply. I must choose to love when hate is easier, when hate is what is expected.[14] My teacher, Jesus, says, "This is my commandment, that you love one another as I have loved you."[15]

When someone is challenging me at the depth of my being, it is terribly hard to make the choice to love her instead of to defend myself, to stay in community with him instead of to walk. It takes a lot of humility to let go of my need to convert the other person to my way of perceiving the world. It takes a lot of courage to allow myself to feel what the other person feels. It takes a lot of strength to continue to work for the world according to my convictions, and not demonize the people who work according to theirs. But I suspect this is exactly what it means to love my enemy. This is hard work, and very few people do it. It is so much easier to argue self-righteously over issues than to learn to listen, to honor, to love. It is so much easier to diminish each other. It is so much easier to dismiss each other.

"Living together in a way that evokes the glad song of Psalm 133 (How good and beautiful it is when sisters and brothers live together in unity...) is one of the great and arduous tasks before (us)," Eugene Peterson writes. "Nothing requires more attention and energy. It is easier to do almost anything else. It is far easier to deal with people as problems to be solved than to have anything to do with them in community."[16]

I have not written this book because I know how to do this. I hate trying to love my enemies. It is the part of Jesus' teaching that I most dislike. I am just like those freedom fighters in Tolstoy's story: I love humankind; it's people I can't stand. To love like Jesus loves demands that I be willing to hang my ego on the cross, that I be willing to give up my self-righteousness, my need to be right,

---

14   Davis, Paul. From a sermon delivered at First Congregational United Church of Christ, Webster Groves, MO, April 8, 1993.

15   John 15:12

16   Peterson, Eugene H. *A Long Obedience in the Same Direction.* (Downers Grove, IL: Inter-Varsity Press, 2000), 179.

my preference for feeling superior, my certainty that I know which side God is on. I do not go easily to that cross.

THE WORD MADE FLESH: LOVE IN ACTION

The Buddhists offer us the image of the *bodhisattva*. A bodhisattva is one who vows not to leave the world, not to claim his or her own reward, until every being, even "the grass itself" reaches nirvana (heaven, bliss, union) as well.[17] The bodhisattva doesn't *have* love, but *is* love itself. The Hindus have a similar concept: for them, an *avatar* is one who has reached the goal and voluntarily sacrifices his or her reward in order to help others reach that place, that state of union. For Christians, the cross can symbolize the sacrifice of the defending ego so that we can be resurrected to a new life in which God's Word—Love—is made flesh and we can live our lives in Christ-like service.

Avatar, bodhisattva, savior: these are models that bring life. How do we embody the reality of God? How do we bring Spirit into matter? How do we live out of our Buddha nature, our true Self instead of our small, false self? How can we be the Body of Christ? How do we incarnate the love of God?

A few years ago, I read a prayer that spoke to me. In fact, it seemed to jump off the page and slap me in the face. It perhaps offers a small answer to the questions I just posed, a beginning step towards our goal of being one with God. It captures how we can begin to love our enemies. Only six words, it is a tiny prayer that packs a big wallop:

O God, bless them. Change me.[18]

That prayer goes against everything in me. Actually, I suspect it is a misprint. What I really want to pray, as long as I'm sure no

---

17 Smith, Huston. *The World's Religions.* (New York: HarperCollins, 1991), 124.

18 Quoted anonymously by Rosemary Cunningham of New York City in *Spirituality and Health*, March/April 2006.

one will hear me, what I really do pray in my heart of hearts is: *O God, bless me. Change them.*

This is our work for the rest of this book (for the rest of our lives). We will explore what it might mean to *bless them* and *change me*. Of all the ideas I could bring forth, I have chosen six: three things we might do if we want to *bless them*, and three things we might do if we want to *change me*. The actions are all simple to understand and practical to implement; you can try them out right away. We'll be a little playful, but we'll also be telling the truth about our lives, and finding ways to live into our convictions a little more than we've sometimes been able to do. It will be a challenging journey, and an empowering one. Let's get started.

WISDOM TO PONDER

If you don't find God in the very next person you meet,
it is a waste of time to look further.
(Gandhi)

Wherever you turn, there is the face of God.
(The Qur'an)

When we judge others, we contribute to violence on the planet.
(Marshall B. Rosenberg)[19]

QUESTIONS FOR REFLECTION AND DISCUSSION

1. Look again at the way we move from accepting someone to naming them enemy, (page 13) This is not a rigid, step-by-step process, but rather an image that helps us see how we accumulate enemies. Can you relate this process to your own experience? Thinking of a specific person or group, see if you can map your version of the steps that took you from welcome to hostility.

---

19 Rosenbaum, Marshall. *Nonviolent Communication: A Language of Life.* (Encinitas, CA: Puddle Dancer Press, 2005), 144

2. In your family, faith community, workplace or nation, whom do you have permission to dismiss, mock or condemn? What group can you slur without being called on it?

3. Consider Vanier's quote on page 16, ending with "True community is different because of the realization that the evil is inside—not just inside the community, but inside me." Does that seem true to you? If so, how is it true of your faith community or other groups to which you belong? What is the external group or situation that your community names as evil? What is the evil within that the group tends not to notice? Try to answer these last two questions again, this time about yourself as an individual.

4. Peterson is quoted on (page 17) as saying "It is far easier to deal with people as problems to be solved than to have anything to do with them in community." Reflect on a time in your experience when you saw someone as a problem to be solved instead of a person to be welcomed and loved.

5. Choose one of the quotes in "Wisdom to Ponder." Which one speaks to you, and why? If possible, share your response with another.

Chapter 2: Bless Them: Pray for Their Well-Being

Many of us have prayed for someone we've named, at least in subtle ways, as enemy. But let's be clear about how we do that. A prayer for another's well-being, a prayer of blessing, does not include praying for their conversion to our beliefs or desired actions. A prayer for another's well-being is completely free of our own agenda. In this chapter, we will look at ways we can do that, including an exploration of this idea in 12 step programs.

Suppose we've been arguing with Mary. We are pressing for acceptance of gay people in our community; she believes the gospel to say something different. This, then, is not a prayer for her well-being: "O Lord, help Mary to become more loving and accepting, to learn that all of us are your children. Help her to move beyond her prejudice and open her heart."

Do you see how there is a lot of vested interest in that prayer? While being loving and open-hearted are good things—and Mary would no doubt agree with us about that—really in this prayer we are asking God to change Mary so she accepts gay people as we do. We are praying that Mary change in a way that she herself does not value. We are assuming that we know what is best for her. And we are being judgmental besides. The unspoken assumption here is that if Mary wants to be more holy, she needs to be more like us.

It isn't always easy to discern when our prayer is really for another's well-being, free of our own agenda. For instance, if our child is using drugs, we feel it is most appropriate to pray that he be healed from his addiction, though he himself might not appreciate that prayer. We don't doubt, in this case, that our agenda is also God's agenda, and is commensurate with our son's long-term well-being. And some would apply the same reasoning to Mary's attitude, believing that accepting gay people is so clearly God's agenda that a change of heart is indeed for Mary's well-being. Discernment will require of us both honesty and humility.

We could pray for Mary's well-being in other ways, and leave in God's hands any possible change of heart. For example, after an intense church meeting about whether or not to welcome lesbians and gays into our church, a meeting in which we were painfully at odds with Mary, we might pray like this: "O Lord, bless Mary tonight; she is probably stressed after this painful meeting. Help her to feel your peace. Watch over her family and bless them with happiness in each other. Protect them and bless them with good health. May Mary know your presence as she works in that garden she loves so. May she feel how much you delight in her."

LOVING-KINDNESS MEDITATION

The Buddhist Loving-Kindness Meditation is a wonderful prayer, too. Here is a simple form of that prayer.

May I be happy.
May I be peaceful.
May I be free.

May my friends be happy.
May my friends be peaceful.
May my friends be free.

May my enemies be happy.
May my enemies be peaceful.
May my enemies be free.

May all beings be happy.
May all beings be peaceful.
May all beings be free.

You can add or substitute other qualities for *happy, peaceful* and *free*; sometimes I've chosen words like *safe, healthy, loved*. Just make sure your words are not efforts to sneak your agenda in the back door, like this:

May my enemies be tolerant.
May my enemies be accepting.
May my enemies be welcoming of all people.

You can add the names of specific individuals for whom you wish to pray:

May Mary be happy.
May Mary be peaceful.
May Mary be free.

When we pray that loving-kindness meditation, we are wishing for our enemies the same thing we wish for ourselves. That is another way to pray for enemies. If in your prayer you are praying for success in your new job, your daughter's improved health, enough money to make ends meet this month, and God's love to go with you through the day, then you could also ask God to bless your enemy with success in his job, healing for his children, enough money to make ends meet, and that God's love go with him throughout this day.

In her book, *An Altar in the World*, Barbara Brown Taylor gives a whole chapter to the practice of blessing others. Pronouncing a blessing, she says, puts you as close to God as you can get.

To learn to look with compassion on everything that is;
to see past the terrifying demons outside to the bawling hearts
within; to make the first move toward the other, however many
times it takes to get close; to open your arms to what is instead of
waiting until it is what it should be; to surrender the justice of

your own cause for mercy; to surrender the priority of your own safety for love—this is to land at God's breast.[20]

Offering a prayer of blessing for one with whom you struggle is a way of sharing in the work of God.

WORKING WITH OUR RESISTANCE

Bless them: pray for their well-being. It didn't take any effort on my part to write that sentence, but I am embarrassed to see how hard it is to live those words. For several months during the time I was working on this book, I was attending a church that was struggling with a serious conflict. I was very angry with some of the people there. We had different perceptions of the issue; I could have lived with that. But their actions hurt me and negatively impacted my ministry in the region; that raised the stakes for me. I had certainly named them as enemy. Before I began working on this chapter, it had never occurred to me to pray for those particular enemies, and as my own words challenged me, I noted my great resistance to doing so.

I find it interesting to explore what that resistance is about. I confess that I get a lot of goodies from naming another as the enemy. How strange it is that there is some gratification, some pleasure, in feeling the victim, in being self-righteous, in blaming. I want to be like Jesus … later. First, I want to be self-righteous. (I am reminded of St. Augustine's wonderful prayer: *O God, make me chaste, but not yet.)*

The people in this church may indeed have acted inappropriately. They may have been living out some unhealthy patterns. My assessment of the situation may have been accurate. When we talk about blessing our enemies, we do not mean that we no longer take stands for or against certain issues and behaviors. The question is whether we can take those stands without demonizing the people who hold the opposite stance. When we find ourselves blaming the

---

20   Taylor, Barbara Brown. *An Altar in the World: A Geography of Faith.* (New York: HarperCollins, 2009) 206.

other, feeling morally superior to the other, or wanting to attack, we have probably demonized our opponent. We need to be wary of assuming we know what is best for our enemy, or that we know what God values. (I think of Anne Lamott's comment, "You can safely assume you've created God in your own image when it turns out that God hates the same people you do."[21]) If you notice that you are patronizing or condescending in your prayer, take that as a red flag that you are probably not praying for the other's well-being as much as you are praying for the other to change to better match your qualifications.

If I have any hope of living what I write about, practicing what I preach, I must be a person of deep prayer. For me, that usually means daily silent prayer. I practice other forms of prayer, too, but sitting in silence allows me to listen. I trust God to be at work in me during that time, honing down my defending ego, my false self, so that my true Self, the Divine within, can be ever more present in my being and my actions.

Some years ago, I spent a week at the French monastic community of Taizé. During a Bible study there one morning, our group leader said something I've never forgotten. He said if we want to be forgiving and have just not been able to do it yet, we can ask God to forgive for us. Perhaps, he suggested, that is what Jesus was doing from the cross when he said, "Father, forgive them." Or in other words, *I can't bring myself to forgive them right now; will you do it for me until I am able to?*

So, I could pray something like this: *Holy One, I am trying to love these people, but I am not managing that yet. Will you love them on my behalf? I'm not able to bless them yet, but I am able to ask you to bless them. Will you bless them on my behalf? And keep working on me.* That might be the first step. Praying for their well-being as best we're able can come next. We can even eliminate words alto-

---

21   Lamott, Anne. *Bird by Bird: Some Instructions on Writing and Life.* (New York: Anchor Books. a division of Random House, 1999), page 22.

gether as we pray, and silently hold the other in the light of God's goodness and grace.

Praying for another's well-being is an important part of Twelve Step programs, coming from work on the Fourth and Fifth step: *Made a searching and fearless moral inventory of ourselves* and *Admitted to God, to ourselves and to another human being the exact nature of our wrongs.*[22] If I were in a Twelve Step program, working through the Fourth Step, I might write a list of all the people, organizations and ideas towards which I hold resentment. It is likely to be a very long list! I would go through each item with my sponsor, who would lead me to see where I am responsible, at least in part, for the difficulty I'm having with the other person or group. Hopefully, I could let go of most of the resentment on my list. But probably there would be a few I still hang on to. Here's where praying for the other comes in.

My sponsor would give me homework. I would be directed to pray, every morning and night, that I might show towards the persons who wronged me the same "tolerance, pity and patience" that I would cheerfully grant to a sick friend.[23] After a few days, my sponsor and I would look at my list again. If there are still names on the list that I have not let go of, we would ramp up my homework assignment. This time I would be directed to pray, morning and night for 14 days, for each person towards whom I am still feeling resentment, anger or hostility. This time I am to "ask in prayer for everything you want for yourself to be given to them…Ask for their health, prosperity and happiness."[24] *Bless them. Change me.*

Rev. Peter B. Panagore, in his book *Two Minutes for God* tells a story that brings home what it means to pray for another's well-being.

After a shipwreck, two men swam to a desert island. Their only hope was to pray. They each sat on opposite sides of the island,

---

22 *Alcoholics Anonymous: The Big Book.* (New York: Alcoholics Anonymous World Service, Inc., 1976), 59-60.

23 Ibid, 67.

24 Ibid, 552.

*each offering their prayers. One prayed for food; a fruit tree ap-
peared. He ate. The other man ate nothing. After a time, the first
man was lonely and prayed for a wife. Soon another ship wrecked,
and the only survivor, a woman, swam right to him. For the other
man, there was nothing. The first man prayed for house, clothes,
food; all was granted. The second man still had nothing. The first
man prayed for rescue; a ship came, he and the woman boarded.
They felt it was ok to abandon the second man; he was obviously
unworthy, since none of his prayers had been answered. Then the
first man heard a voice from Heaven. "Why are you leaving your
friend behind?"*

*'My blessings are mine; I prayed for them. His prayers were
not powerful enough. He got nothing."*

*"You're wrong! He had only one prayer, which I answered. If
not for that, you'd have received nothing."*

"What did he pray for that I should owe him anything?"

"His only prayer: that your prayers be answered."[25]

Perhaps you can see that praying for our enemy's (or, on some
days, our beloved's) well-being requires some inner work on the
ego, the part of us that wants us to be always right, always the
winner, always the best. Each of the six tools in this book will bring
us back to this place. Being a person of peace requires a profound
inner transformation: a dying of the old ego self so we can be
transformed into a new being. God blesses us with community to
sustain us on the journey towards compassion. God blesses us with
enemies to get us going in the first place.

---

25   Panagore, Rev. Peter B. *Two Minutes for God.* (New York: Touchstone
     Faith, 2007), 214.

WISDOM TO PONDER

> *A great Sufi teacher told of the time when Jesus went for a walk and was insulted by some town folk. Jesus responded by including these town folks in his prayers. "Why didn't you answer their insults?" a disciple asked. Jesus replied, "I can only pay people back with the coins I have in my purse." (source unknown)*

> *If you want to see the brave, look for those who can forgive. If you want to see the heroic, look at those who can love in return for hatred. (Hindu scripture: Bhagavad Gita)*

> *We depend on the other in order for us to be fully who we are... [this is] the concept of Ubuntu: a person is a person through other persons. (Archbishop Desmond Tutu[26])*

QUESTIONS FOR REFLECTION AND DISCUSSION

1. What has been your experience with praying for your enemy? Have you done that often? Do you find it difficult? Does your own agenda seep into your prayers? If you have been able to pray sincerely for your enemy's well-being, what enabled you to do that?

2. Think of a person who upsets you, one whom you've perhaps named enemy, at least in your heart. Using prayer beads, offer prayers for their well-being, one bead at a time, one blessing per bead. How far along your string of beads can you get? If you wish to share this exercise with a partner, pray your beads aloud so that your partner can hold you accountable for offering prayers that do not further your own agenda. Then, of course, switch roles with your partner.

---

26   His Holiness the Dalai Lama, Archbishop Desmond Tutu, Douglas Abrams. *The Book of Joy.* (New York: Avery, an imprint of Penguin Random House, 2016), 60.

3. Buddhist monk and teacher Thich Nhat Hanh says, "The practice of deep looking makes peace possible."[27] How do you understand the practice of deep looking? What does that mean to you? Reflect on a time when you practiced deep looking, even though you may not have thought of it in those terms. Perhaps you've been able to practice deep looking towards a small child, your beloved, or a dear grandparent nearing death. Have you ever practiced deep looking towards someone you did not like, or even someone who threatened you? If not, what prevented you from doing that? If so, what empowered you to do that?

4. Choose one of the quotes in "Wisdom to Ponder." Which one speaks to you, and why? If possible, share your response with another.

---

27 Hanh, Thich Nhat. *Creating True Peace.* (New York: New York Free Press, a division of Simon & Schuster, 2003) 10.

Chapter 3: Bless Them: Be Willing to Feel at Least a Little of My Enemy's Pain

I occasionally worship with First Congregational United Church of Christ in Memphis, Tennessee. Worship there is a beautiful and powerful celebration. Each service ends with an affirmation of faith written by the congregation. The affirmation includes this line: "We will let ourselves begin to feel at least a little of the pain of those we have considered our enemies." The first time that I shared that affirmation with those Memphis folks, I was startled. I had never thought of such a thing: allowing myself to feel some of my enemy's pain. Who would want to do that? And why?

Using Defenses to Protect Ourselves from Pain

Rather than allowing ourselves to feel our enemy's pain, or even our loved one's pain, we build up strong defenses. (Often, they serve to keep us from feeling our own pain, as well.) We stay in our heads, that is, our intellects, instead of opening our hearts. We keep so busy that we can't give much time or attention to one who is hurting. Instead of listening to the other's story of pain and loss, which might touch our hearts, we problem-solve for them, or break in with our own story. We respond to stories of hurt or injustice with cynicism or blame. These are some of the defenses we have accumulated to protect us from feeling another's pain.

The 20th century writer James Baldwin says, "I imagine one of the reasons people cling to their hate so stubbornly is because they sense once the hate is gone they will be forced to deal with pain."[28]

---

28 James Baldwin, *Notes of a Native Son*. (Boston: Beacon Press, 1955), page 101.

Hating is pretty easy, really (though it does significantly drain our energy). Choosing to love is harder. It takes a lot of courage to allow oneself to feel someone's pain, and particularly the pain of one we have named enemy. Most of us never do that. If we felt their pain, we might not be able to keep them in the role of enemy anymore.

It is hard to feel another's pain if we are not in touch with our own. If we are serious about praying *bless them; change me*, we might have to look honestly at what we do with our own pain. (Here we are again at that hard inner work.) We have many medications to deaden our pain: drugs of all kinds, alcohol, food, television, shopping, overwork, fast pace, addiction to social media, overbooked schedule. These are effective defenses against facing the grief we've never resolved, acknowledging our addiction, dealing with the unhealthy, unhappy dynamics in our marriage or the emptiness of our spiritual life. A deepening prayer life will require that we look at what he have tried to avoid looking at and deal with what we see. It will require that we face our particular "drug" of choice for avoiding those situations and emotions we don't want to face.

CHOOSING COMPASSION

Dealing with our own pain nurtures our compassion. We accept someone else's hurt because we finally accept our own. We know that the pain need not destroy us. We are less judgmental of others as we become less judgmental of ourselves. We have the energy to look at someone else's pain because we are not using up all our energy trying to hold back our own.

Marshall B. Rosenberg, in his book, *Nonviolent Communication,* talks about behaviors that block compassion. He lists moralistic judgments; classifying; analyzing; labeling; determining wrongness; comparing; communicating our desires as demands; thinking based on who deserves what; and denying our own responsibility.[29] Each of these very common behaviors serves as a defense against feeling the other person's pain. Each, by the way,

29 Rosenberg, Marshall B.. *Non-Violent Communication.* (Encinitas, CA: Puddle Dancers Press, 2005),16-22.

will also alienate the other person, whether he or she is your enemy or your beloved. The alternative to blocking out another's pain is compassion, but compassion is dangerous. It can steal our enemies from us. In, *if the Buddha married*, Charlotte Kasl invites is to face our opponent—enemy or beloved—and remember: This person wants what you want: to be loved, to be free of suffering, to experience joy.[30]

We were talking about being willing to feel another's pain… that's called compassion…at a workshop in Iowa one Saturday, and I appreciated one man's comment: what we want to offer is empathy. Sympathy is not the same. We can offer sympathy from a safe distance. Empathy, on the other hand, implies getting inside another's skin and feeling his or her pain. Sympathy is nice, but it is empathy that heals.

I want to be the kind of person who lives out of compassion, but the truth of my life is that I hold grudges, I nurse resentments, and I hang on to enemies as though I needed them. I suppose I think I do need them: they keep me from facing the shadow side of myself. I guess I hold grudges because I like that delicious feeling of superiority. Sometimes I nurse my anger because my victim status has some nice perks. And I'm not so good at forgiving. If I let in my enemy's pain, I might have to let go of that superiority and that victim status. I might have to do my own inner work. I resist that. I am one of the people Richard Rohr talks about: "We seem to think someone else is always the problem, not me. We tend to export our hate and evil elsewhere."[31] But God is a God of abundant mercy, and instead of judgment, I feel God's warm, loving, empowering grace, enabling me to take the next step, however small, towards peace.

Many years ago, I played flute in my high school band, and I had worked up to the coveted position of first flute. I enjoyed that

---

30   Kasl, Charlotte. *if the Buddha married*. (New York: Penguin Group USA, Inc., (2001),16.

31   Rohr, Richard. *Things Hidden: Scripture as Spirituality*. (Cincinnati, Ohio: St. Anthony Messenger Press, 2008), 133.

honor and responsibility for only about six weeks when my family moved to another state, and in the band at my new school, I began over again, lowest flute in the ranking. One moved up in the rank by a system of challenges, challenging a player of higher rank on a particular piece of music that both players would perform for the band director. One day we were given a new piece that included a difficult flute solo. Each of the flutists was overwhelmed…except me, because I had played that piece in my previous school. I, too, had been overwhelmed when I first saw this solo, but over time, with my teacher's help, I had finally learned it. I thought of a way to ease my hurt about no longer being first flute: I challenged the first flutist on this piece, this piece which she had just seen, and which I had known and played for months. Of course, I kept to myself the secret that I already knew this piece. The challenge was set for a week or two later. She was appalled. I was delighted, and smug. At least, I was delighted and smug for a few days. Then I began to feel uncomfortable. I pushed those feelings away as best I could, but like dandelions in a perfect lawn, they kept popping up. Finally, I had to acknowledge that I felt guilty, but I was pretty skilled at ignoring that, too, or rationalizing how what I was doing was perfectly legal…which it was; legal, but not ethical.

What began to crack my greed (for first place in the flute section) and self-righteousness was that I was haunted by the look on Betsy's face, that look that I saw when I challenged her to this very difficult music that she had just seen for the first time; that look that I saw each day in band practice when she looked stressed and sad and discouraged. Despite my best defenses, I began to hear the voices in my head that asked, "What do you suppose she is feeling?" I was beginning to get in touch with a little bit of my enemy's pain.

Finally, one day, by the grace of God, I found the courage to call her—hands shaking as I placed the call, voice shaking as I talked—to cancel the challenge, and confess to her that I had been unfair because the music was not new to me, and I had played that difficult solo before. *Oh God, bless them. Change me.* Betsy was, by the way, enormously gracious, more than I deserved. She remained our band's first flutist and I didn't challenge her again.

If we decide to be willing to feel a little of another's pain, we let our defenses down a bit. We relate from our hearts as well as our heads. We acknowledge the ways we might be blocking compassion, and make some changes in ourselves. We stop our busyness, ignore call waiting, close our laptop, turn off our smart phone, and be fully and totally present another's story, even if it is hard to listen to. If we choose to bless our enemy, this is a powerful way.

WISDOM TO PONDER

> *If we could read the secret history of our enemies, we should find in each person's life sorrow and suffering enough to disarm all hostility.* *(Henry Wadsworth Longfellow)*

> *You can't shake hands with a clenched fist.* *(Indira Gandhi)*

> *Hatred can never put an end to hatred; love alone can This is an unalterable law.* *(The Dhammapada, Buddhist scripture)*

QUESTIONS FOR REFLECTION AND DISCUSSION

1. How did your childhood family deal with pain? Which part of those patterns have you carried into your adult life? Which ones are helpful? Which ones are not?

2. What is your "drug" of choice in dealing with pain? Finding ways to ease pain is a good skill. Using those ways to excess to avoid pain is not. Which of your tools for dealing with pain do you feel are helpful and healthy? Which tools might you want to reconsider?

3. Look on page 32 at Rosenberg's list of behaviors that block compassion. Which of these have you experienced

in someone's listening to you? What was your response? Which of these do you use most often in listening to others?

4. Share an experience in which you were able to feel an enemy's pain. What was that like for you? What made it possible to open your heart?

5. Choose one of the quotes in "Wisdom to Ponder." Which one speaks to you, and why? If possible, share your response with another

CHAPTER 4: BLESS THEM: CHERISH THEIR STORY

If you listen to the conversations we have with one another, you will notice that we don't always cherish someone else's story, and certainly not the story of our enemies.

The Oxford Dictionary defines cherish this way: *to protect or tend lovingly, to hold dear, to cling to.* We can cherish a child, cherish the soft old shawl our beloved grandmother made so long ago, cherish our dream of teaching children with disabilities.

When we are newly, delightfully in love, we cherish our beloved's story. We want to hear everything that happened and everything he feels. We want to understand, to know, to share. It isn't hard to do that, because our love has opened our hearts. But somehow, after we've lived together for ten years, it is not so easy. He is still our beloved, but now we are busy and we think we know all his stories and frankly, he is a bit irritating, and sometimes more than a bit, to tell you the truth. Somehow, we didn't notice that when we felt the passion of new love. And there is that woman at church; she is really a challenge. She goes on and on, and we pretend to listen while planning how to end this conversation as quickly as possible. Given how challenging such encounters are, why even try to cherish the stories of our enemies? They've got their story all wrong, anyway. They don't need someone to cherish their story; they need someone to correct it.

So, our track record at cherishing—protecting, tending with love, holding dear—another's story (their feelings and hopes and experiences and world view) is spotty at best. Let's see if we can find some tools that might make it easier for us to *bless them* by cherishing their story.

The first step is to recognize how we listen, and how we fail to. We must bring our communications patterns into the light of our awareness. Think of a time when you were talking to someone about an issue or feeling important to you, and though he or she claimed to be listening, you did not feel heard or understood. Can you articulate anything that your listener was doing or failing to do that contributed to your frustration at not being heard? What was it about your listener's behavior that made you feel he or she was not cherishing your story? Most of us can think of such an example easily, because we have so many of them. We want so badly for someone to listen deeply to us. When that doesn't happen, we feel angry or depressed, and behind that anger or depression is a deep loneliness, a sense that no one knows us or understands us or perhaps even loves us. Good listeners are rare.

And we know that we ourselves are not very good at listening, either. It is always easier to see the speck in another's eye and miss the log in our own, so to recognize the patterns that prevent us from cherishing one another's story, we began by remembering an incident in which someone failed to cherish us and our story. But let's not stay in that judgmental place. In any situation, the one thing we can always change is ourselves. How is it that we fail to cherish another's story, even when we start out with the best intentions? Here are some ways.

FAILING TO CHERISH THE OTHER'S STORY

When we give unsolicited advice, we are failing to cherish another's story. Giving advice is saying "If you were as smart as me, you'd see this obvious solution. But since you aren't and didn't, and I am and did, I'll help you."

When we problem solve, we are failing to cherish another's story. There is a time for problem solving; sometimes it is just what the other person wants. We go to professionals like doctors or attorneys or electricians for the purpose of getting our problems solved. However, listeners very often resort to problem solving because they are bored (let's move this along; I have important things to do) or they are trying to keep the speaker's pain from touching themselves. We may not want to hear about their scary symptoms because it opens our fear of serious illness. We might not want to walk with them through the story of their daughter's alcohol problem because it threatens our efforts to keep our spouse's addiction a secret. We might not want to listen to their despair at the state of the world, because we are trying to hold back the flood of our own despair. So, to avoid feeling any of the other's pain, we attempt to solve their problems. The effect this has on the speaker is often powerful. It immediately ends the conversation (which was perhaps our real, though unconscious, agenda.) The speaker recognizes that here is one more person with whom it is not safe to share honestly.

It is clear that we are not cherishing the other's story when we fidget, check our watch, or let our eyes wander to the computer screen while our companion is talking.

We fail to cherish another's story when, as they are speaking, we are planning what we will say as soon as we have a chance to break in. Or maybe as they speak, we are planning our grocery list. We can get pretty skilled at saying "Really? Oh, dear!" in all the right places.

Sometimes when our friend is sharing his feelings with us, we respond with "You shouldn't feel that way!" That is rarely felt as support; it is often experienced as judgment. Feelings just are, and we feel what we feel. What we do with those feelings is something else again, but there is no judgment in having them. When Jesus taught us to love our enemies, perhaps he meant our inner enemies, as well, the parts of ourselves that we don't like, such as our anger or jealousy or fearfulness. In this context of accepting and respecting all our feelings, even the ones we don't want to have, I appreciate the poem "The Guest House" by 10th century Persian poet and Sufi holy man Rumi, translated by Coleman Barks.

This being human is a guest house,
every morning a new arrival.
A joy, a depression, a meanness,
some momentary awareness comes
as an unexpected visitor.

Welcome and entertain them all!
Even if they're a crowd of sorrows
who violently sweep your house
empty of its furniture,
still, treat each guest honorably.
He may be clearing you out
for some new delight.

The dark thought, the shame, the malice,
meet them at the door laughing,
and invite them in.

Be grateful for whoever comes,
because each has been sent
as a guide from beyond.[32]

We fail to cherish our friend's story when we tell him not to feel what he feels.

Of course, any kind of judging or evaluating, whether of another's feelings, values, convictions or actions, is a failure to cherish another's story. That does not mean anything is ok. We are bound to prevent another from committing violence. Wrong-doing needs to be named. People must be held accountable, not just by authorities but also by peers. But as listener's, we begin by listening, not judging. Father Greg Boyle, in an On Being interview with Krista Tippett, reminds us that compassion involves "a decided movement towards awe and giant steps away from judgment." He speaks of

---

32 Barks, Coleman. with John Moyne. *The Essential Rumi*. (New York: HarperCollins Publishers, Inc., 1995), 109.

a compassion that "can stand in awe of what people have to carry rather than judgment as to how they carry it."[33]

When we correct another's story, or interrupt to set her straight, we may be failing to cherish her story.

And here is a very familiar one: when we break into another's tale to tell our own, we are failing to bless, failing to cherish. I call this stealing the story. Suppose your neighbor is telling you of her weariness and discouragement at caring for her elderly mother. You might respond with "I know just what you mean. For five years my elderly aunt lived with us, and let me tell you…" and you are off with the details of your own woes. Empathy is good. Revealing briefly that you have had a similar experience and it brought forth similar feelings can be very helpful to your neighbor, but only if you limit that connection to a sentence or two, and then turn the conversation back to her story. Of course, sometimes the conversation is best when it goes back and forth, and it is appropriate to do so. Stealing the story becomes an issue when your neighbor needs to share her pain, and you are short-circuiting that process.

You may recognize most of these behaviors, as I do; we sometimes act in these ways when we are listeners. I lift up these failures at listening, which become failures at cherishing, so that we can recognize them. If you want to work a bit with these, here's a good exercise. First, spend a day or two noticing when others show any of these behaviors towards you. Notice what they do; notice how that makes you feel. Or when you are in a group, notice how people do these things to one another. Don't correct anyone; just notice. This part of the exercise—seeing the problems out there—will be easy.

The next step is harder: determine that for one week you will notice each time you use one of these behaviors. You are not going to try to change your behavior; your task is simply to notice when you fail to listen, fail to cherish. A vital part of this exercise is not judging what you are noticing. Check those inner voices that jump

---

33   Boyle, Father Greg. On Being interview with Krista Tippett, November 23, 2015. Quoted in Weavings, A Journal of the Christian Spiritual Life, Volume XXXI, Number 4, Aug/Sept/Oct 2016, p.41

in with "See! There you go again! You are a first-class jerk! And you thought you were a good person!" Instead, just note the behaviors: "Oh. I just stole the story" or "Problem-solving" with no judgment attached. The first step toward making changes is just to bring your actions into the light of awareness.

CHERISHING THE OTHER'S STORY

So, we've talked about how we as listeners can fail to cherish someone's story. Let's move on: how do we cherish another's story? Here are some ways.

- We listen.

- We make eye contact.

- We stay in the present moment, focusing on the other.

- We express empathy.

- We ask for more.

- We honor confidentiality.

- We ask clarifying questions instead of making evaluative comments.

- We allow silences to be there, without rushing in to fill them.

- We offer only those comments or questions that will take the speaker deeper into her story or her feelings.

- We listen with our hearts open, as best we can.

So now we have a list of some things that prevent us from cherishing another's story, and some things that help us to do so. If you have spent some time noticing when other's fail to cherish someone's story, and then some time noticing when you do, you might feel ready to practice one of the behaviors that allows you to cherish another's story. If you want to work at cherishing the story, I suggest that you focus on just one thing on our list of ways to cherish the other's story, so that you are not overwhelmed,

Perhaps you have tried to do this—intentionally practice even one behavior that will allow you to more fully listen and cherish—with people in your family, your co-workers, friends at church. If so, and if you are ready for a greater challenge, try it with someone you don't like. Try it with the person who is against everything you are for. Try it when you are talking with another about something that pushes your buttons. This will be very difficult. Everything in you will cry out to defend your position, and to correct, or even attack, the other person and her sadly incorrect ideas. You will learn a lot about yourself by observing your reaction to your effort to cherish an enemy's story. You will get some (unwanted) practice in humility.

Jonathan Haidt, in his book *The Righteous Mind: Why Good People are Divided by Politics and Religion*, writes that we don't change people's minds by rational discussion. People make decisions quickly, based on sentiment, intuition and life experience, and only later do they find reasons to support the decisions they have already made. If we hope to persuade people, we need to appeal to their emotion or intuition. Before trying to convince someone that we are right and they are wrong, we would do well, Haidt says, to ask ourselves, "Why do they believe this way?" Everyone has a reason for what they do. Haidt uses liberals and conservatives as an example. People who identify themselves as liberal value change and variety, compassion and fairness. Those who identify as conservative will also value compassion, but most important to them will be stability and order, loyalty and authority. In any community, both change and stability are needed. One is not good and the other evil. When we recognize that, perhaps we can stop trying to conquer others; instead, we will be open to learning from them. We might even be willing to cherish their story.

Once I was in Michigan at an inter-faith conversation arranged in the hopes of helping people of faith to grapple with issues around the hot topic of homosexuality. Two speakers, each a leader in a local faith community, had been asked to dialogue together about this subject. The two represented opposite ends of the spectrum on this issue. I was very disappointed in the conversation, and I doubt that anyone left with any deeper understanding than they came with. Neither speaker cherished the story of the other. Neither one tried to understand why the other person held the convictions that he did. They didn't even listen to one another very well. Each waited with obvious impatience while the other spoke, apparently giving attention only to what they themselves planned to say. There was no real dialogue. There was nothing to make us look at this sensitive issue in new ways. There was no wisdom offered that would help us to hear or understand another's view, and thus live peacefully together. There were no stories or insights that allowed us to open our hearts. What was the point?

In one of my classes on this material, one man said he had trouble with the word cherish. He could handle *respecting* the other's story, but how could he *cherish* it? Did that mean he had to embrace values that were abhorrent to him? Was he supposed to pretend to support something that he opposed? Those are fair questions. At the beginning of this chapter, I repeated the definition of cherish, and one part of that is *to protect*. That might be helpful here. We cherish someone's story when we protect their right to feel what they feel, to come to the conclusions their life experience has led them to, to feel safe to share their values and perspectives, trusting they won't be attacked. Perhaps the benefit of using *cherish* in this somewhat startling way is that it catches out attention and reminds us that we are working with ideas that are very counter-cultural, ideas that will stretch us enormously, ideas that defy our reason, our common sense. We are not talking about just being a nice person. We are talking about growing into the Buddha nature or Christ consciousness. We are not talking about just changing a habit or two; we are talking about transformation of our whole being.

Listening in an open-hearted way does not mean that you agree with the position that the other is putting forth. You will have opportunities to state your differing convictions at another time. But if we are interested in furthering peace, we can begin by learning to listen to our enemies and our loved ones in such a way that we genuinely cherish their story. That means we encounter the other, not as an opponent to overpower, but as a human being who hurts and hopes just as we do. The Jewish teacher Emmanuel Levinas says that we are not converted by ideas but "by the face of the other."[34]

I am not very good at this. My ego wants to defend my ideas. I get some satisfaction out of showing the other person that he is wrong. I like feeling superior. But when I have been able to do this, I find that I can't attack anymore. I still disagree with the other's position, but now I have a sense of her humanness, of his hopes and fears, which are so like my own. When I reach even this first step towards the place of compassion, I am ready to do the work of Christ.

EMPOWERED FOR CHERISHING

If you have read this far in this book, you may feel tired by now. We've talked about a lot of ideas, a lot of challenges, and a lot of hard work. Many people try to be good people, try to live without violence, but they don't make life harder than it is by trying to love their enemies. I mean, it's one thing to decide you will not harm others, or steal from them, or bear false witness, or try to ruin them on purpose. But to actually try to love them, to bless them, to forgive them, to understand them, for God's sake: that is unreasonable. It's too much. It may not even be possible.

34 Quoted in Richard Rohr. *Things Hidden: Scripture as Spirituality.* (Cincinnati: St. Anthony Messenger Press, 2008), 179.

I have felt that. In Chapter 2 of this book, I referred to a time when I was caught in a conflict in the church I attended. It was during the time I was working on the manuscript of this book. I had set the goal of working on it a couple hours every day, but instead I didn't open this file for four months. I was too discouraged. I felt unable to do any of the things I was writing about. Not only was I unable to bless my enemies, I didn't even want to. I was big into vengeance. I didn't want to cherish their story or feel their pain or pray for their well-being; I wanted to destroy them (politely, of course; I didn't want it to look bad for me.) I wanted to hurt them. I was full of hate and anger and I didn't know what to do with it. How could I possibly write this book? For four months, I didn't.

The only admirable thing I did during that period was to recognize that the kind of person I was being was not the kind of person I wanted to be. I didn't judge that much, but I kept noticing it. God, I suspect, is very patient. I found it very hard to pray for the well-being of my enemies, though I did sometimes try. But even then, I felt hypocritical: in my heart, I didn't mean it, and Spirit and I both knew that. But I remembered the Twelve Step wisdom: *fake it until you make it*, so I tried again.

I failed pretty totally at being willing to feel a little of their pain; I didn't see that they even had any pain. I could only see the pain they were causing my family and me. Most of the time, I just let that be, acknowledging in my prayer and to my friends that I was not loving my enemies, nor even wanting to, but I was able to honestly say that I wanted to want to, sort of.

I knew that Jesus is very big on forgiveness, but I began to accept that forgiveness is a process that moves slowly, one little step at a time. That was not an excuse to avoid working on it, but it was a decision not to add to the violence in the world by beating up on myself. I often prayed for help. "God, this is the best I can do today. It is not very good. If I am going to grow in my capacity to love, you need to work on me some more. I can't do this on my own. The ball is in your court."

I made it a point during that time to read stories about people who had loved their enemies, people like Nelson Mandela and Corrie ten Boom and Desmond Tutu and Dorothy Day and early Quakers. I read the writing of Anne Lamott, who struggles like I do, and makes me laugh about it. I began, after a time, to notice which friends fed my anger and self-righteousness, and which ones, while never judging me, helped me to see what the next step towards the light might be. I sought out the helpful people more often. Whenever I found myself spinning the bad guys (them) good guys (me) story over and over in my head, I began to recite the 23rd psalm instead, or St. Francis' prayer. I also came to realize that for me, for most of us, it is so imperative that we do this work in community because it is much too hard to do alone.

I also try to remember that I can always take the next small step, even though I may not feel capable of walking the distance. Once I was in Montana leading a workshop on this material, and during a break a woman asked to speak with me. She suffered from severe depression, and she knew that in her current state, she could not put much energy into this challenging work. She didn't want to leave the workshop feeling guilty that she wasn't doing more. I appreciated her comments. When we suffer from depression or illness or grief or loss, we need to be gentle with ourselves. Those times already push us into the deep inner work of transformation; it may not be wise or possible to challenge our souls to more at this time. Being perfect is not our goal. Sometimes one small step is good enough.

Perhaps what helped me the most to move towards loving, even though I couldn't quite reach it, was that I trusted. I trusted myself, I think, to move beyond my hateful attitudes in time. I trusted Spirit to help me and heal me. I trusted my friends to understand and support both my anger and my desire to be like Christ. I trusted my community to hold me to the gospel standard, to lift me up when I faltered, to hold me accountable, and to love me through it all. And I trusted the Risen Christ to stay with me, to stand as a witness to what is possible, even for me, to light my way out of the darkness in which I was, for the time being, caught up.

In time I returned to writing this book, not because I could do all that I was writing about, and not because the simple ideas I offer will eliminate every conflict in my life, or yours either. I returned to writing because I needed a book like this.

I know we're all welcome at the table, but do I have to sit next to you? How do we stay in community with the people who drive us crazy? With the people who are for everything we are against? How do we work for the peace we sing about? We are looking at the little prayer: *O God, bless them. Change me.* Of all the things we could do to *bless them*, we have focused on three: pray for their well-being; be willing to feel a little of their pain; and cherish their story. Now it's time to consider the second half of our prayer: *change me.*

WISDOM TO PONDER

No matter how far you have gone on the wrong road, you can turn back. (Turkish)

It is not how much we do, but how much love we put into the doing.
It is not how much we give, but how much love we put into the giving. (Mother Teresa)

In the struggle between the rock and the water, in time the water wins. (Chinese)

QUESTIONS FOR REFLECTION AND DISCUSSION

1. Practice listening with a partner. Partners A and B agree on a sensitive, hot button issue about which they have opposite convictions. Partner A shares her convictions while B listens. After a few minutes, A reflects on how she experienced B's listening. Then reverse roles.

2. Find a book on communication and read the sections on listening skills. Some titles are listed in the Selected Bibliography. You might arrange a session on listening skills for your church or your book club.

3. Author and church historian Diana Butler Bass writes "The unanimous witness of the ancient fathers and mothers was that hospitality was the primary Christian virtue."[35] How is cherishing another's story an act of hospitality?

4. Someone has pointed out that *anger* is only one letter away from *danger*. It is nearly impossible to cherish another's story if we are coming from a place of anger. What is your relationship with anger? When has it been useful, and when has it been harmful? Sometimes we repress our anger; that often turns to depression. Sometimes we throw our anger out into the world, hurting others and adding to the violent energy of the world. Can you think of a third option for dealing with anger? Have you tried it? If so, how has it worked for you?

5. Choose one of the quotes in "Wisdom to Ponder." Which one speaks to you, and why? If possible, share your response with another.

---

35 Bass, Diana Butler. *A People's History of Christianity*. (New York: HarperCollins, 2009), 62.

CHAPTER 5: CHANGE ME: BE WILLING TO BE VULNERABLE

Charlotte Kasl, in her book, *if the Buddha married,* writes "We speak in the spirit of revealing ourselves, not changing our partner."[36] That's a very optimistic statement. I suspect that most of us, most of the time, speak in the spirit of changing our partner. Certainly, when we speak to those who oppose us on issues of illegal immigrants or gun control, we speak in the spirit of changing our opponent.

However, if we have decided to try to live this small prayer, *O God, bless them. Change me*; if we have decided to be a peace-maker in this way, then we need to consider the first of our *change me* examples. We need to be willing to be vulnerable.

Being vulnerable in front of loved ones is often very hard. Being vulnerable in front of enemies seems unheard of, and we can't help but notice that some of the ones who have done so (Jesus, Gandhi, Martin Luther King, Jr., for instance) got killed for it.

And yet, we recognize that when we protect our vulnerability, using our many fine-tuned defenses, the other person or group is sure to remain an enemy. It is our defenses that make us attack one another. Sometimes it is not appropriate to be vulnerable, and our defenses are very important; we'll talk more about that shortly. But most of us live almost totally out of our defenses; we go through life living out of our defenses. The Bible calls that hardening our hearts. When our hearts are hardened, neither compassion nor communion can happen.

Jesus was vulnerable and died on the cross. On the third day, according to Christian belief, he rose from that death into a greater life than he had known before. There are many ways to understand

36 Kasl. *if the Buddha married.* 23.

those events; that story carries many layers and levels of truth. One thing we learn from the story of Jesus' crucifixion and resurrection is that giving ourselves away in love (read *being vulnerable*) leads to new and greater life. We could also see Jesus on the cross as a model of a love that is free of a defending ego. In our effort to live like Jesus, we could decide to let our defenses down and be willing to be vulnerable. Let's see some examples of how we might do that, and then talk about why we might choose vulnerability.

CHOOSING TO BE VULNERABLE

When I listen without jumping in with my counter-arguments, I am being willing to be vulnerable. Listen for the word "but" in your conversation. If you are saying, "Yes, I understand that, but..." you are not listening with an open heart; you are bringing out your weapons. Marshall B. Rosenberg, teacher and author of *Nonviolent Communication*, urges us to listen with empathy rather than put our "but" in the other person's face.[37] Think of an issue that pushes your buttons. Can you imagine yourself listening to one who holds the opposite convictions, listening without having to defend or prove, listening for the human person behind the conviction, for the experience, the pain, the joy that led her to that conviction? Can you imagine listening without needing to share your perspective, at least at this time?

When we talk from our hearts instead of just our heads, sharing our feelings instead of only our thoughts, we are being willing to be vulnerable. I was leading a Bible Study one evening, and we were reading a powerful and challenging passage. I asked the group to tell me what they felt after hearing those words. I clarified that I didn't want to hear what they thought, but only what they felt, and if they began to share a thought, I would interrupt them. The first person to speak began with "I think that..." I interrupted her and repeated my instructions: feelings, not thoughts. The next person said, "I feel that this image meant something different in Jesus'

---

37   Rosenberg. *Non-Violent Communication*, 119.

time." I stopped him; he began the sentence with "I feel" but his sentence was still a thought. No one in the class was able or willing to respond with a feeling.

In our culture, we are very skilled at expressing thoughts, but less so at expressing feelings, especially expressing them in appropriate ways. Traditionally this has been harder for men than for women. If you think this is an issue for you, find a list of feeling words and study it a bit. You can find such a list in books on communication or in Twelve Step literature. How often do you use those feeling words? How expansive is your feeling vocabulary? What might happen if, in an argument with your beloved, instead of repeatedly defending yourself, you said in the midst of the fray, "I'm scared. I'm scared that our relationship is at risk." Being willing to be vulnerable is one way to diffuse a situation.

When I am willing, during a difficult encounter, to lay down my defenses (such as my arrogance, my self-righteousness, my cold, unemotional demeanor), I am being willing to be vulnerable.

When I allow myself to feel at least a little of my enemy's pain, I am being willing to be vulnerable.

When I am willing to feel my own pain without blaming someone for it, I am choosing to be vulnerable.

Jean Vanier, founder of l'Arche communities, writes a lot about vulnerability because his life work is with vulnerable ones, people with grave disabilities. But he writes not just about their vulnerability, but about his own, and ours.

> *All my life I had been taught to climb the ladder, to seek promotion, to compete, to be the best, to win prizes. This is what society teaches us. In doing so, we lose community and communion… (Then one day) I discovered something which I had never confronted before, that there were immense forces of darkness and hatred within my own heart…I did not want to admit all the garbage inside me. And then I had to decide whether I would just continue to pretend that I was okay and throw myself into hyperactivity, projects where I could forget all the garbage and prove to others how good I was. Elitism is the sickness of us all. We all want*

to be on the winning team. That is at the heart of apartheid and every form of racism.[38]

Climbing the ladder, being the best, throwing ourselves into hyperactivity, elitism: these are some of our defenses against vulnerability. It takes a lot of courage to allow oneself to be vulnerable. It takes wise discernment to know when being vulnerable is helping to dismantle our defending ego, when it is furthering peace in the world (or at least our little corner of it) and when being vulnerable is foolish and serves no good purpose. The reason this is so important is because of what happens when we don't deal with our own pain. Buddhist monk and teacher Thich Nhat Hanh says "When we cannot handle our suffering, we spew forth our frustration and pain onto those around us…we hurt others while we are in pain. We—each of us—must become responsible for our own pain."[39]

LOGS AND SPECKS

As I ponder Vanier's words about elitism, about our always wanting to be on the winning team, I am reminded of an experience I had a few years ago. I was in a gathering of church folks, mostly moderate to progressive Christians. The speaker who addressed us that day was informing us of what the religious right was doing. As soon as he began, I became uncomfortable because his talk was shaped around an us-and-them attitude. There were good guys and bad guys. I began to take notes as he spoke. I wrote down the convictions that he claimed (and I agreed) the religious right held. He was putting these items on the table as a means to caution us to be wary of the right. What concerned me is that he never acknowledged that we, the religious moderate and the religious left, held the very same convictions. For instance,

> *We don't have to listen to them, because they have nothing to teach us.*

---

38   Vanier. *From Brokenness to Communitiy*. 18-19.
39   Thich Nhat Hanh. *Creating True Peace*. 14.

We are right, and God is on our side.

We are trying to gather voters so as to influence the outcome.

We want judges who will uphold our values.

We try to teach people how wrong their perception is.

He shared fourteen such statements, openly critical, and I was amazed that no one else in that gathering spoke up to say that the moderate and liberal corners of the faith believe, say and do the same things. We take a different stand on the issues, but our attitudes and tactics are similar. All of us, progressives and fundamentalists and conservatives and liberals and evangelicals: we have all learned the lessons taught to us: that our enemies are more violent than we are, that they are probably beyond change, and that God is on our side. I appreciate Richard Rohr's insight: "The ego diverts your attention from anything that would ask you to change, to righteous causes that invariably ask others to change."[40] Somehow, I kept thinking about logs and specks. Focusing on our issues more than on our enemy's issues is another way to be appropriately vulnerable.

I am reminded of the old feminist wisdom: you can't use the master's tools to dismantle the master's house. What are the master's tools? An us-and-them mentality, arrogance, accusatory language, stereotyping, proof texting, feeling superior, not honoring or listening to the other: these are some of the master's tools. One who takes any of these stances is certainly not coming into the conversation with any vulnerability. Jesus modeled one way that leads to transformation, and it has to do with being vulnerable more than being right. It is more about community than conquest.

The conversation at that meeting reminds me of nations at war: I'll line up my weapons and fire; I'm doing that for the sake

---

40   Rohr, Richard. *The Naked Now: Learning to See as the Mystics See.* (New York: Crossroads Publishing Co., 2009), 94.

of God and country. You'll line up your weapons and fire; you're doing that because you are evil. Where is the peace in that?

Ronald Rolheiser, in his book, *The Holy Longing*, reflects on our willingness to hold tension as an important part of our faith and our prayer.

> *(I)t is good to carry tension and not resolve it prematurely because, ultimately, that is what respect means. By not demanding that our tensions be resolved we let others be themselves, we let God be God, and gift be gift.*[41]

He goes on to say that when we carry tension, we are allowing a gestation process to unfold: we have the opportunity to turn hurt into forgiveness, anger into compassion, and hatred into love. I think these are vital points for those of us trying to learn to love our enemies. When we must quickly label everyone as bad guy or good guy because that resolves the tension within us, we are not letting others be themselves, and we are not allowing the time needed for hurt to turn into forgiveness or hatred to turn into love. If we are willing to live with the tension that one of God's beloveds is for what we are against, that our opponent can take the stand she has and still be a very good person, then we make room for Spirit to move. Being willing to hold tension, to refuse the temptation to resolve our inner discomfort too quickly, makes us feel vulnerable.

I always learn from my students (more, I often suspect, than they learn from me). When I was sharing this material with one class, a woman reminded me that if we are going to talk about vulnerability, and sharing pain, we need to acknowledge cultural differences. I had not thought about that, but she is right. Some cultures value the stiff upper lip, the silence about pain, the keeping on keeping on. Traditionally the English have been like this. Other cultures value open emotion, freedom to share intense feelings. Latino cultures are often this way. So, when we invite ourselves to

---

41   Rolheiser, Ronald. *The Holy Longing: The Search for a Christian Spirituality*. (New York: Doubleday, 1999), 223.

be vulnerable, we need to acknowledge that will mean different things according to the culture.

WHEN VULNERABILITY IS NOT APPROPRIATE

A willingness to be vulnerable can be an important tool for building peace. But if we're going to talk honestly about vulnerability, we must deal with some of the issues that vulnerability raises. What about domestic violence? What about vulnerability that is forced upon us because there is a power difference or gender inequality in the situation in which we find ourselves?

First let's confess that we are always tempted to use safety as an excuse not to live the way of peace. The threats of danger in our world may mean we take certain precautions and set certain boundaries, but it does not excuse us from the universal spiritual commands to welcome the stranger and love our enemy.

We also acknowledge that most of us are not called to be martyrs, and though we may occasionally be called to risk our physical safety for a greater good, that call is rarely part of our ordinary days.

When we are in a conflict situation with someone who appears to have more power than we have (facing an abusive spouse or a belligerent boss, or being the only woman in a male-dominated office, for example), we add creative thinking to our bag of tricks. Maybe we can find an advocate to join us in the conversation with our doctor. We can choose not to be in relationship with one who abused us. Sometimes the wisest and most loving act is to leave the situation. Maybe we can get our colleagues to agree before beginning the conversation that the person with the least power sets the rules. Maybe we want to make a conscious choice not to respond in kind, not to get the drama going. Maybe we can think of something to make the situation safer before we act.

When we pray *O, God, bless them. Change me*: be willing to be vulnerable, we are talking about vulnerability that is freely chosen. When we are vulnerable because of someone else's behavior, we are still bound by the command to love enemies, but we may choose to do so in other ways than exposing our own vulnerability.

Most of us are pretty gentle, peaceful folks. We don't understand why there can't be peace in the world. I feel that I can't expect peace in the world if I can't even pull it off in my neighborhood, or in my church community, or at my breakfast table. Peace begins with me. I don't know how to bring peace to the world, but I can begin right now to look at how I live my life. *O God, bless them. Change me* is a way to begin. And one way to change me is to notice how often (how rarely) I am willing to be vulnerable.

WISDOM TO PONDER

> *We belong to a larger reality than our own ego self.*
> (*Pierre Teilhard de Chardin*)

> *If I say I am working for peace, but am myself angry and self-righteous, then the energy I am putting into the atmosphere is anger and self-righteousness. If I come preaching the gospel of Christian love but am myself rigid and judgmental, I am putting into the atmosphere rigidity and judgment.*[42]
> (*Cynthia Bourgeault*)

> *A prophet models: witness to a non-violent God; forgiveness; simplicity of life; and community beyond differences.*[43]
> (*Ron Rolheiser.*)

QUESTIONS FOR REFLECTION AND DISCUSSION

1. What are some of the defenses you use to avoid being vulnerable?

---

42 Bourgeault, Cynthia. *Mystical Hope*. (Cambridge, MA: Cowley Publications, 2001), 91.
43 Rolheiser, Ronald. *Secularity and the Gospel: Being Missionaries to Our Children*. (New York: Crossroads Publishing Co., 2006)

2. Share a situation from your life in which you or someone else defended themselves against being vulnerable. What happened? What was the outcome? Share a situation from your life in which you or someone else took the risk to be vulnerable. What happened? What was the outcome?

3. I have suggested that one way to view the passion story is to see Jesus as modeling the death of our defending ego, and the new life that comes from that. What do you think about this interpretation?

4. Consider Thich Nhat Hanh's words from "Logs and Specks" on page 54, "We—each of us—must become responsible for our own pain." How would one do that? What would it look like, to become responsible for our own pain? How do you do that?

5. Choose one of the quotes in "Wisdom to Ponder." Which one speaks to you and why? If possible, share your response with another.

CHAPTER 6:
CHANGE ME: REFUSE TO
DIMINISH ANOTHER PERSON

To diminish someone is to make him less than he really is. We can diminish people to their face, behind their backs, or in our own minds. To diminish a person is a kind of violence.

Let's name some of the ways we diminish another person. Sometimes in our minds we reduce someone to a one-dimensional being. She has a disability; that becomes our defining characteristic of her, even though we could describe her in many other ways. He is African-American and that's all we see of him; we reduce his opinions to "Well, being black, of course he'd think...." We put him in a box because he is a Republican, or make up our mind about her because she is lesbian. When we define a person primarily through one trait, we are diminishing them.

When we assume we know what is best for another person, we diminish him or her. If the other is trapped in an addiction, or suffering a deep depression, or still a child, we may well know what is best; we may know better than he or she does. But most of the people we encounter are as competent as we are, and yet we still assume we know better than they do what is best for them. This is a way of diminishing another.

When we dismiss his ideas because he's over 70, or don't ask her input because she is an artist and you know what they're like, we are diminishing another person.

We diminish another person when we don't know their culture, and so we judge them based on our culture.

We diminish our partner when we assume she is wrong, when we feel superior to her. We diminish our neighbor when we stereotype him or label him.

To dismiss someone is to diminish him or her. In his book, *Healing the Heart of Democracy*, Parker J. Palmer writes some strong words about such dismissals:

> *Within me is a power of darkness that may tempt me to want to "kill you off" when you threaten some concept of reality or morality that I cherish. I will not do it with a weapon but with a mental dismissal, some way of putting you into a category of people whose opinions mean nothing to me. Now I no longer need to be bothered by your otherness or by the tension it creates in me. That, it seems to me, is the spiritual equivalent of murder: I have rendered you utterly irrelevant in my life.*[44]

SEEING THE PROCESS AT WORK

"...to render you utterly irrelevant in my life." How easily we do that! One evening I joined a discussion group at our local library. A topic was chosen at each meeting, and participants joined in discussion and debate, following some ground rules about respecting one another. The man in the green shirt sitting on my left began to dominate the conversation. He prefaced his opinions with statements like "Anyone who has studied this knows this to be true" and "This is not my opinion; it's fact." He condemned one of the world religious traditions as being inherently evil. I felt his manner to be arrogant, and he didn't give others much chance to speak. In very short order, he had pushed most of my pushable buttons. I dismissed him almost immediately. Even so, I could hardly stay in the room with him. I stopped looking at him as he spoke. I realized I even shifted in my chair so that I subtly turned away from him. I had to make an effort not to convey on my face the disrespect and

---

44   Palmer, Parker J. *Healing the Heart of Democracy: The Courage to Create a Politics Worthy of the Human Spirit.* (San Francisco: Jossey-Bass, 2011), 127.

disgust I was feeling. And then I thought about my efforts to write this book.

My first perfectly logical reaction was to decide to quit writing this book. Obviously, I can't do any of the things I'm writing about, so give it up.

My second thought was that I just wanted to be like everyone else, and hate people and feel superior and, yes, diminish them without having to worry about it. Loving your enemies takes way too much work.

Then I began to wonder: just in case I were going to keep writing a book on a subject like this, just in case I were going to make a stab at loving my enemies—no promises, but just in case—how would I deal with the man in the green shirt? What might I do?

The setting put limits on the possibilities, which offered good practice, because often the situation or the relationship does limit our options. I didn't know this man, would not necessarily ever meet him again. We were in a group that had an agenda and time limitations. So, was there anything I could have done instead of diminishing this person, as, in my heart, I certainly did?

The first thing that I think of was to give some attention to myself. Why had he (unknowingly, of course) pushed my buttons? Why had his comments stirred so much energy in me? Could I listen to him, disagree with his comments, even recognize some poor communication patterns in his words, and just observe them calmly, without judgment? To be without judgment would not have precluded my challenging his ideas in appropriate ways, or expressing my own ideas in contrast to his. I might have even said "I am uncomfortable when you say...." I can practice discernment without judgment. Why did I need to judge him, anyway?

The next week, I decided to return to the group at the library just to see if I could react differently to the man in the green shirt. Could I disagree with him without dismissing him? He came in after I was seated, and took a seat right next to me. I could feel myself bristle. But I took my attention from him (he wasn't speaking at that moment) and focused on myself. Did I need to react so strongly? I calmed. Later when he was speaking, I tried to listen without judgment. That was difficult. Then I noticed that I was holding my breath. I realized that every time he spoke, I unconsciously held my breath. I remembered Cynthia Bourgeault, who says in her book, *The Wisdom Jesus,* "Never do anything in a state of internal brace—that is, in a state of physical tightness and resistance...."[45] I was holding my breath because I had gone automatically into a state of internal brace—tightness and resistance. All I needed was that awareness, that recognition of what I was doing, and I began breathing again. I consciously slowed and deepened my breathing. I found then that I was able to listen without so much inner judgment. I still disliked what he was saying, but my buttons weren't getting pushed. I was not giving energy to resistance. I could disagree with him without moving into fight mode. I wasn't cherishing his story yet, but it was a start.

If you listen, you will find that we diminish other people in many of our conversations. When I have led a workshop on this material, after the lunch break I repeatedly hear people say that I've ruined the conversation around the table because the participants are hearing how much of their normal every day conversation violates one of our six teachings, especially this one. They can't think what to talk about anymore!

AHIMSA

It is especially hard to recognize when we diminish another, because we are given permission to do this. Every group we belong to gives us permission to hate, judge, or diminish some other group. A new family moved into town and asked if this town was particularly prejudiced. "Why do you ask?" a neighbor questioned. "Well, my wife is black and Catholic, and I'm a Polish Jew. We have a lesbian daughter, and our son is a practicing Buddhist." The

---

45   Bourgeault, Cynthia. *The Wisdom Jesus: Transforming Heart and Mind—a New Perspective on Christ and His Message.* (Boston: Shambhala Publications, Inc., 2008),173.

neighbor replied, "Oh, you're welcome here, I reckon. But you sure won't hear any jokes."

There are people we are allowed to hate, people we can tell jokes about, and get a laugh. There are people we can gossip about in the parking lot before church, and then listen to the gospel without qualms. Each of us gets permission to hate someone. Progressive communities may regard evangelicals as being less mature in the faith. Traditional churches may regard liberal church folks as being unfaithful. A meditation group that prides itself on being welcoming may still hold a tacit list of types of people who, they feel, don't really fit in, and would not actually be welcome.

Hindus use the word *ahimsa*, which may be translated as non-violence or non-harming. If we want to nurture world peace, if we want to live in healthy communities, we must practice *ahimsa*. Jainism, another ancient religion in India, shares with Hinduism this commitment to *ahimsa*. The Jain code of conduct has five principles: to practice non-violence in thought, word and deed; to seek and speak the truth; to behave honestly and never take anything by force or theft; to practice restraint and chastity in thought, word and deed; and to practice nonattachment, non-acquisitiveness. This is very like ethical codes from other religions.

The value of looking at ethics through another tradition is that it is not familiar, and so we hear it anew. Perhaps that enables us to see that when we diminish another person, we violate at least four of those Jainist principles.

Sometimes we talk about others behind their back. Maybe we could consider *ahimsa* instead. Sometimes we do a lot of blaming. That's a good time to remember *ahimsa*. Sometimes we stereotype someone. *Ahimsa* is called for; maybe we could practice it, even a little. *Ahimsa* is about gentleness. It is about looking at a situation or person with compassion instead of judgment. It's about refusing to diminish another person.

By the way, we might want to acknowledge here that we also diminish ourselves, and the more we do that, the harder it is to avoid diminishing others. Do you blame yourself excessively? Do you name yourself klutzy, stupid, inept, ugly? Those are ways of diminishing yourself, a violation of *ahimsa*.

O God, bless them. Change me. What a challenge this little prayer presents! It requires that we practice humility; that is not one of our favorite stances. Benedict of Nursia, a 6th century Christian saint, wrote the Rule of St. Benedict, which has shaped the life of religious communities for more than 1500 years. He quotes James 2:13 when he instructs us to "Always let mercy triumph over judgment."

Ahimsa. Refuse to diminish another person.

WISDOM TO PONDER

> *The supreme religious challenge is to see God's image in one who is not in our image. (Rabbi Jonathon Sacks)*

> *The truth you believe and cling to makes you unavailable to hear anything new. (Pema Chodron)*

> *Love your enemies. Do good to those who hate you. Bless those who curse you. Pray for those who persecute you. Do to others as you would have them do to you. Do not judge. Do not condemn. (Jesus, according to Luke 6)*

QUESTIONS FOR REFLECTION AND DISCUSSION

1. Whom are you allowed to hate? Consider your family, your circle of friends, your church, workplace and nation: in each of these communities, whom can you diminish (judge, hate, stereotype, gossip about) without anyone calling you on it? Are there other people or groups that your communities do not allow you to diminish? What is the difference?

2. Do you diminish yourself? In what ways? Why?

3. When have you felt diminished by someone? How did that feel? How did you respond (outwardly or internally) to that experience?

4. Can you remember a time when you diminished someone else? Share that experience with another person.

5. Choose one of the quotes in "Wisdom to Ponder." Which one speaks to you and why? If possible, share your response with another.

CHAPTER 7: CHANGE ME: TALK FROM MY FEELINGS INSTEAD OF MY THOUGHTS

We come to the last of our three efforts at *change me*: talk from my feelings instead of my thoughts. This does not mean that we never have a rational, intelligent conversation about ideas. But when we are trying to understand another person, to honor them, to practice peace, this is worth looking at.

At the Christian community of Taizé in France, people from all over the world gather to pray. Everyone attends daily Bible studies during their stay at Taizé. Some of the visitors are liberal and some are fundamentalist. Some read the Bible literally and some do not. Every denomination and nation is represented. You can imagine the potential for argument! The rule at Taizé when I was there was this: in discussing the Bible, we were to talk about our experience, not our ideology. We were to talk about our feelings, not our thoughts. This worked. I learned that week that ideas and opinions invite conflict, but experiences (our stories and our feelings) invite compassion.

Suppose you identify yourself as pro-choice. In a debate at a church meeting, what happens inside you when someone says, "The gospel of Jesus makes it perfectly clear that abortion is a sin. Any Christian who knows the Bible will see that." What response arises in you?

Imagine that the same person says this instead, "I feel Jesus' love for me and for all people, and it is that love which has led me to believe that abortion is a sin." Did that statement stir any different response in you? In both examples, the speaker expressed strong conviction and you, being pro-choice, will still differ with the speaker. But one version probably generated a hard response (anger, defensiveness, desire to argue or to end the conversation) and the other a gentle response (respect, willing to continue the dialogue).

Here's another example. Suppose you are concerned about the refugees who are hoping to enter the United States to escape war and persecution, and you want to express your opinion. Then you remember that you are trying to talk out of your feelings instead of your thoughts. So, you say "I feel that we should not let more refugees enter our country." Are you talking out of your feelings? No, that is still a thought, an opinion, an idea. To speak out of your feelings requires a little practice, and some courage. You might say, "I am scared about our letting in so many refugees. I wonder how that will affect our jobs and our neighborhoods and our values. I want to be compassionate, but I worry about how much they will change our nation." You are taking responsibility for your own feelings, and you will probably be met with less hostility.

So, one way to change ourselves in our effort to grow in love is to talk out of our experience, not our belief systems, out of our feelings, not our opinions.

LEARNING A NEW VOCABULARY

Sometimes, in order to do that, we need to learn a vocabulary of feeling words. You can find these in books on communication or in Twelve Step programs and literature. Some of us need to practice being able to identify our feelings, and playing around with a list of feeling words can help.

If that is easy for you, here is a graduate course in expressing feelings. Marshall B. Rosenberg suggests that some words seem like they express our feelings, but they are actually our interpretations of another's behavior.[46] These are not useful, and will not promote peace. Consider these examples of words we commonly use to express what we feel: abandoned, abused, attacked, betrayed,

---

46   Rosenberg. *Non-Violent Communication.* 42-43.

boxed-in, let down, patronized, taken for granted, used. When I use one of these words (usually when I am angry), they do, in a sense, express what I'm feeling. But I can see that they really lay blame on someone; they are my interpretation (and judgment) of another's behavior. Do you see that? As I said, this is a graduate course in expressing feelings. I may indeed have been abandoned; that might be fact. It might be important for me to name that honestly with my pastor or therapist or friend. But if I am in conversation with someone and my goal is to regard the other with compassion, I might do better to use non-judgmental words. I can say, "I felt dismayed when you weren't there. I felt so hurt when I had to face this alone." Those sentences communicate truth, but they are only naming what happened and what I felt; they are not interpreting the other's behavior. Indeed, this step is challenging, and not the place you want to begin. But I have found it worth my attention.

COPING WITH INTENSE FEELINGS

As long as we're talking about feelings, let's take a moment to talk about what we do with the feelings we carry about hot issues or hostile situations. If, in our effort to be responsible Buddhists or nice Christians or faithful Muslims or good people of any or no faith tradition, we stuff down the fear or hurt or anger we feel, we will find it very difficult to practice blessing the other or changing ourselves. We must find a safe way to vent some of those feelings so that we have the inner space we need to act out of wisdom and compassion. Let me share some ways I have done that so that you might be encouraged to find appropriate ways that work for you.

After suffering a major house fire which destroyed more than half of everything we owned, including many irreplaceable family treasures or heirlooms, I felt great anger. Some friends began saving glass bottles for me, and several times I took a carton full of glass to the recycling center and threw each of the bottles into the metal bins, putting all my anger into that throw, taking satisfaction from the noisy, destructive shattering of glass. That helped a lot. When

I didn't have any glass, I went into a county park with a carton of eggs and threw eggs, one at a time, at trees. The physical energy of the throwing and the visible mess helped, yet that action was safe and insects or the next rain would kindly clean up the harmless mess I'd made.

My spouse once served as pastor of a church that got caught in a conflict which eventually centered on the pastor. Finally, there was a difficult meeting in which my spouse was asked to resign. After that meeting, several friends from the church came home with us and spent a few hours not only allowing us to vent, but venting with us, which felt very helpful. As we sat down together to share lunch, we prayed. We promised Jesus that we'd return to our efforts to love our enemies very soon, but that afternoon we were going to let all the "nastys" have free rein. We suggested that maybe he didn't want to listen! We did vent and blame and judge and rage for several hours, and when they all left, my spouse and I felt drained, calmed, supported, and open to thinking more clearly and allowing the possibility of understanding, forgiveness and compassion to reappear.

The next day, as friends and family called to ask how the meeting went, I told the story, still with considerable anger, over and over. For me, when anything difficult has happened, telling the story repeatedly is part of the healing. It is part of getting the anger or hurt out so there is space for love and forgiveness. A dear friend of mine, one who has listened patiently to so many of my stories, says that a friend is one who will listen to your story over and over again until you don't need to tell it anymore.

It is important to honor whatever you feel, to let it have center stage in safe and appropriate ways, whether that means throwing eggs at trees, telling the story, writing in a journal, chopping wood or playing a fast, hard game of tennis. We do that to make space. Intense anger, like intense grief, takes up a lot of room. It fills our bodies and souls until there seems to be nothing in us but the anger or the grief. How could there be room for anything else, like love or forgiveness or understanding? All the suggestions in this book are about making space: making space for Spirit to work, making space for a new idea, a new way of interacting, making space for the indwelling Christ to be heard, making space for the Buddha nature to emerge, making space for *ahimsa*, making space for other options for handling conflict, making space for transformation. Be aware of when you are so crowded with anger that there is no space for anything else, and find appropriate ways to make room.

In this chapter, we talked about a third option we might choose if we prayed *change me*: talk from our feelings instead of our thoughts. We have now looked at three actions we might take if we want to *bless them*, and three if we want to *change me*. We could, of course, have chosen many other options, but these six give us plenty to work on. In our final chapter, we'll talk about how we get empowered for this hard but vital work.

WISDOM TO PONDER

> *No matter which spiritual path you choose, the nuts and bolts of transformation wind up looking pretty much the same: surrender, detachment, compassion, forgiveness.*
> *(Cynthia Bourgeault)[47]*

> *Shall I not inform you of a better act than feasting and prayer? Making peace between one another.*   *(Muhammad)*

> *Love is meaningless which does not cherish in others the freedom to be different from ourselves.*   *(Source unknown)*

QUESTIONS FOR REFLECTION AND DISCUSSION

1. Consider a controversial statement that is spoken as a thought, an opinion. Can you reword the statement so it says the same thing, but is spoken as a feeling? Here are some statements to practice on.

---

47 Bourgeault, Cynthia. *The Wisdom Way of Knowing.* (San Francisco: Jossey-Bass, A Wiley Imprint, 2003) xvii.

    a. We obviously need stricter gun control laws.

    b. It is wrong to refer to God as Mother.

    c. Given the terrorist threat, we should ban Muslims from coming to the U.S.

    d. Climate change must be our primary concern.

2. Choose one feeling word, perhaps angry or happy. How many words can you list that describe that feeling? What different things might you feel if you are angry or happy?

3. Look again at Rosenberg's comments on page 70-71 that distinguish true feeling words from words that interpret another's behavior. What do you think of that distinction? Does it make sense to you, or not? When you have used one of those words, or witnessed someone else doing so, what was the result?

4. Choose one of the quotes in "Wisdom to Ponder." Which one speaks to you and why? If possible, share your response with another.

CHAPTER 8: SAYING YES TO TRANSFORMATION

I have led retreats based on this material many times, and I always get a very positive response, but I rarely find out whether participants work with the material in their own lives once the retreat enthusiasm wears off. In my own church, people still talk about these ideas, and challenge one another about them, several years after we shared the retreat. I know this material has haunted me and empowered me. I often question whether I can continue to preach and teach about loving your enemies when I myself am so poor at it. Perhaps it is my four grandchildren, to whom I have dedicated this book, who keep me at the work, not just the preaching and teaching, but the work of opening myself over and over to God's transforming power. I want a better world for Joshua and Lucy and Jessica and Ella, a world of less violence and more love, a world of gentle strength, a world where forgiveness and respect and laughter are in plentiful supply.

And so, in this chapter, I offer some ideas about how we might be empowered to love our enemies when it is so much easier not to bother.

BE IN COMMUNITY

The best tool for empowering me to bless them, change me is to live and act and grow in community with others who are trying to do the same thing. I have several communities, and they all offer vital support. There is my church. I hear there the words of scripture, and the connection to our 21st century world. I am challenged to live beyond my self-serving ego. I sing hymns whose words remind me who I am, whose I am, and how I choose to be.

I sing and pray and laugh and cry in the midst of others who are making the same commitment to love and understand and welcome that I am making. This community keeps me at it.

And I have a community of friends, great people who are also committed to lives of peace and understanding and non-violence. They, too, are doing the work I'm doing. They are not judgmental, this dear community of friends, so when I call one of them and vent my great anger at some situation or person that has challenged me, they don't scold. They don't offer platitudes. They receive my fury with an open heart, knowing that in time I will move beyond blame and rage and self-pity and delicious fantasies of vengeance. They trust me. They trust that I am headed in the right direction and I'll get there. And if I should get stuck in the rage, their trust in me helps to move me forward.

My family is another community that sustains my efforts to be a Christ to those I meet. Like my friends, they sustain me with their love and trust. My elders sustain me with the example they modeled for me, and my children and grandchildren sustain me because I am always thinking about what I want to model for them. Is this the kind of person I want them to be? If not, I'm inspired to change my behavior. Is this the kind of person Dad was? If not, I want to look again at my behavior.

Do you have in your life the kind of communities that can sustain you in the work of outer peace and inner transformation? Do you have communities that can forgive you when you fail, that will love you back to your best self? If you don't, maybe you could begin to build them in your life. Maybe it is time to get back to going to worship every week. Maybe you could invite some others into a book study. Anne Lamott's collections of essays deal with some of these issues in ways that are humorous and non-judgmental; that is an easy place to begin. Wendell Berry is another great essayist whose books can help. A Bible study on the Sermon on the Mount (Matthew 5-7) or on the Gospel of Luke will offer plenty of opportunity to talk about our efforts to stay in community with those we wish would drop off the face of the earth. Maybe you could start a "love your enemies" group, in which you meet monthly to pray for the world and share with one another some current personal struggles to welcome or forgive or listen, share with the intent of supporting and empowering one another in this work. Could you initiate, at your faith community, school, workplace or civic group, some sessions on communication skills, emphasizing non-violent communication and conflict resolution? Marshall B. Rosenberg's books are great tools, or you may have resources at a local seminary, peace institute, mediation center, Buddhist community, or college.

You might also find community among the peace and justice activists in your town. Be aware, however, that there are different approaches to peace work. Gandhi and Martin Luther King, Jr. modeled for us doing peace work from a foundation of faith and commitment to something beyond ourselves, even something beyond our worthy goals. Some who work for justice and peace focus on their goal and lose sight of the bigger picture, so that their attitudes are judgmental and their actions include various sorts of subtle violence. This will not be a helpful community for those of us committed to the inner transformation of the arrogance and violence within ourselves, those of us who want to be a Christ to one another, or those of us who have committed ourselves to any of the world's great spiritual traditions and their ancient wisdom.

The voices of culture are so pervasive that unless you have other voices speaking to you regularly, you will start buying into the voices of culture. So, use your discernment, but don't try to do this work alone. You need community.

BE IN PRAYER

Prayer is our primary connection to Spirit, to the empowering God, to the indwelling Christ. For a person of faith, prayer is the first and foremost tool for discipleship and for inner transformation. There are many ways to pray. I just bring to your attention the prayer form par excellence: silent meditation. All of our world faith traditions lift this up as the most important spiritual practice. In my tradition, Centering Prayer is a popular and easy to learn method of silent prayer, though there are others as well.

Other traditions also offer good models for meditation. We have many misconceptions about silent prayer, misconceptions that cause many people to give up. You do not need to sit in an unusual posture and not move. You will not be able to spend twenty minutes without thoughts, and the expectation that you are supposed to do so programs you for failure. Sometimes you'll feel something lovely after your silent prayer, like inner peace or God's love or presence. Very often you won't. Your emotions are not a measure of whether your prayer is "good" or "effective." This prayer that goes beyond words and images will, over time, transform you, but if that is to happen, you must do the practice. It is the best foundation for your faith journey and your ability to love when it is hard.

You can also pray with words, of course. You can ask God's help with loving. You can rant in prayer about what so-and-so did to you, and what you'd like to do in return: plenty of psalms model that kind of prayer for us. You can humble yourself before God, confessing how inadequate you are to this task. You can read printed prayers, letting their language speak for you. You can, as we talked about in Chapter 2, pray for your enemies. Whatever form you choose, use it. Pray a lot.

PRACTICE PATIENCE

To help you stay in community with people who are a challenge for you, you can be part of a supportive community and you can pray. You can also have patience with the process. It takes a lot of slow to grow.

Theologian Stanley Hauerwas says that the politics of peace is the politics of time, and peace is just another name for patience.[48] He quotes Paul Virilio who says the dominant form violence takes in modernity is speed.[49] If you are serious about transformation, about journeying with Jesus, about becoming a Christ to others, about living out the Buddha nature, you will have to practice patience: patience with other people, who change so much more slowly than you want them to, patience with yourself, as you discover over and over that what you know and what you do don't always match, and patience with God, who does not run the world the way you think God should.

Have patience, and have patience with others. Once you learn some new ways of being in the world, some better, more loving ways, it will be hard to watch the folks around you who don't know those ways, and who are not very loving. It is entirely possible that your spouse may not appreciate hearing that since you've read this book, you see how inadequate he or she is in getting along with others. It is entirely possible that your boss might not appreciate your pointing out the error of her ways. There may be times when you can help others by sharing some of what you're learning, but be careful. Allow others to grow at their own rate. And patience is called for, again, because if you make a serious conviction to stay in community in healthy ways with challenging people, you may discover that is sometimes a lonely place to be.

You will get all inspired by this book or some speaker, and go back to your life certain that you'll finally be able to welcome your irritating sister-in-law. That feeling remains strong…until your next encounter with her. Then you blow it. This is a process. Learning, or being reminded, of some new ways of living with other people is a first step. Remembering those ways in the heat of an encounter,

---

48 Hauerwas, Stanley and Jean Vanier. *Living Gently in a Violent World.* (Downer's Grove, IL: Intervarsity Press, 2008) 47.

49 Ibid, 50.

and then, if you do remember, having the courage to try them, are more steps. Figuring out what didn't work, despite your best effort, so you can tweak your best effort, is yet another step. It's a process. It takes time. Be patient with yourself. Be patient with your failures. Be patient with your heart in those times when you don't want to welcome or understand the other, when you don't want to be a Christ in the world, when you are too angry or too tired. Be patient.

START SMALL

At workshops on this material, I encourage people to choose one of the six tools we talked about, just one, and commit themselves to working with that one, just one, for a month, just a month. (Too much? Commit to one week.) Start small. After all, you are, at the same time, trying to do a better job at recycling, eat more leafy greens and fewer donuts, and remember to floss your teeth. You can only hold so many challenges. So, start small. One useful way to begin is to choose one area—say, refusing to diminish another person—and decide that you will observe your own and other's interactions for a week. You won't try to change your behavior, to give up your ways of diminishing another; all you'll do for a week is observe. Remember not to judge yourself. Just note when and how you diminish someone, and then let it go. This is a very effective step that will make you ready to work later changing some behavior. Another way to start small is to choose one person or environment that offers you a little challenge, but not too much. You might decide to try to cherish the story of that talkative woman at church who is a little bit annoying. See if you can do that with her, and practice there before you try it on your ex-spouse.

USE HUMOR

Community, prayer, patience with the process and starting small: those are tools to help you. And then there is humor. Don't take it all too seriously. Don't take yourself or your failures at loving your enemies too seriously. Laugh more often. Be intentional, if need be, to incorporate into your life funny reading, comedy films, friends with a great sense of humor. Laughter is healing and re-energizing, but more than that, it is a reminder that it isn't all up to you: not saving the world, not transforming your own life. It isn't all up to you. God is at work and grace happens. Laughter is your statement of faith, confessing that you believe in grace.

***

A rabbi asked his students how they could tell when night had ended and the day had begun. "Is it when you see an animal in the distance and you can tell whether it is a sheep or a dog?"

"No," answered the rabbi.

"Is it when you can look at a tree in the distance and tell whether it is a fig tree or a peach tree?"

"No," answered the rabbi.

"Then, when is it?" the students demanded.

"It is when you can look on the face of any man or woman and see that it is your sister or brother. Because if you can't see this, it is still night."

O God, bless them, and let me help you. I will pray for their well-being, free of my own agenda. I will let myself feel at least a little bit of my enemy's pain. I will cherish their story.

O God, change me, and let me help you. I will find the courage to be vulnerable. I refuse to diminish another person, starting now. I'll talk from my feelings instead of my thoughts.

O God, help.

I wish you well on your journey of peace-making. I am making that same journey. I trust us to grow into, to live out of, the spirit of Christ. On behalf of my grandchildren, of all our grandchildren, I thank you for being willing to do this work. I know that you are held tight within God's grace.

I know we're all welcome at the table. And I trust that someday soon, we'll each be willing to sit next to whoever comes to join us. May it be so.

WISDOM TO PONDER

> *The ultimate religious question today is not "How can I find a gracious God?" but "How can we find God in our enemies?"*
> *(Walter Wink)[50]*

> *Transformation has to do with the way the walls separating us from others and our deepest self, begin to disappear.*
> *(Jean Vanier)[51]*

> *Don't assign difficulty undue importance.*   *(Rolf Gates)[52]*

QUESTIONS FOR REFLECTION AND DISCUSSION

1. This chapter suggests several tools that can help us to do this work:
    a. Be in community with others who are doing this work also.
    b. Pray.
    c. Have patience.
    d. Start small.
    e. Hang on to humor.

---

50 Wink, Walter. *Engaging the Powers.* (Minneapolis: Augsburg Fortress, 1992) 263.
51 Hauerwas, Stanley. *Living Gently in a Violent World.* 26
52 Gates, Rolf and Katrina Kenison. *Meditation from the Mat: Daily Reflections of the Path of Yoga.* (New York: Anchor Books, 2002) 64.

2. Which of these might help you? Which ones have you experienced, and what were the results? What would you add to this list?

3. This book offers 6 things we might do if we wish to work for peace, if we wish to increase our capacity to love. Which of these six were particularly helpful to you? Would you add any to the six presented here? What would they be?

4. Has your study of this book changed anything in your perspective or your behavior? If you are comfortable doing so, share your experiences of transformation that relate to your work on this material.

5. How might you share this material with others in your faith community or book club or civic group?

6. Choose one of the quotes in "Wisdom to Ponder." Which one speaks to you and why? If possible, share your response with another.

PART 3:
INVITING OTHERS TO JOIN US AT THE WELCOME TABLE

A Leader's Guide: Using This Material in a Class, Workshop or Retreat

I encourage you to share this material with your communities, and I want to make it as easy as possible for you to do that. In this section, I offer some guidance and suggestions to help you prepare a program based on this book. Then I give you possible schedules for using this material in a one-day workshop, an overnight or weekend retreat, or a 6 or 8-week class. Finally, I help you turn the contents of this book into a class or workshop involving discussion and activities.

Consider where you might offer this: in your faith community, in your meditation or prayer group, in a gathering of high school youth, in men's or women's groups, in spiritual formation retreats. You might combine this program with a potluck or a concert of chamber music, choir or praise band.

Now let's see how we might make this happen in your community.

THE SETTING

Space is very important! It will affect the energy of your class or retreat. If the room is comfortable, attractive, cozy, and appropriately warm or cool, participants will relax. An intimate setting (if the size of the group allows) will encourage deeper sharing. This might mean the chairs are in a circle or semi-circle, or tables are arranged in a horseshoe shape or some way that allows people to see and hear each other. The energy and engagement will be much reduced if the room is too hot or too cold, if the acoustics or sound system is poor, if the seating is uncomfortable.

You will want to think about what seating works best for you. Do you want people to sit at tables? This makes writing easier, and gives folks a place to put their coffee cups and other belongings. But it may feel less cozy, and make it harder to hear one another. Sitting in chairs arranged, for instance, in a semi-circle makes communication easier, but requires balancing notebooks and cups. Sitting in rows, one behind the other, is the least ideal option because people can't talk with each other as easily, and that arrangement tends to encourage the participants to be passive while the leader teaches. But if that is the only option you have, you can make it work if you are aware of the limits and compensate for them.

Have water, coffee, tea and perhaps lemonade available throughout the session. Some groups like to have simple snacks as well. When you are welcoming the group, make them aware of the beverages, and invite them, if you wish, to help themselves any time during the session. Or you may prefer to ask them to visit the snack table only at the beginning and end of each session, and at break times.

It is helpful to have books for participants to browse, especially books that are on the resource handout that you will give them. This peaks their interest in the subject, and allows them to look at books before they decide whether to buy certain titles. Some groups choose to sell books, as well. The money from such sales might help to pay expenses, thus lowering the cost (if any) for participants. Or it can be used to support the faith community or organization sponsoring these sessions. Or you might choose to donate the money to some group or cause that reflects the subject of these sessions, such as a local peace center.

In this book, there are three quotes at the end of each chapter. You could print some of those to hang around the room.

In a central place, create a focal point or altar that is visually nurturing. You can cover a small table with a beautiful fabric. Candles are lovely. A live green plant is nourishing to the spirit, as are cut flowers. (I prefer to use live plants or bouquets though I recognize artificial ones may be cheaper and more convenient. Growing things offer us a healing energy.) If yours is a faith community, you might wish to have a symbol to recognize that: a cross or a small statue of Buddha, for instance. Maybe you have a Tibetan singing bowl to set there. Or decorate your table with sea shells, pine cones, rocks. You might have a picture of someone who lived out the theme of this event, like Gandhi or Dorothy Day. Make this focal point soothing, beautiful, meaningful. You can also do this on a smaller scale on each table, if the participants are seated at tables.

Here are some ideas that fit in the "above and beyond" category. They are not essential, but I have found that they add a lot. I prepare the room and the meal, if there is one, as though the participants in the workshop were guests at a spa. It is a luxury for many folks to be offered beauty and comfort, to be pampered. Not all the ideas I suggest will fit your style, your energy, your budget or the number of volunteers you have to work with, but perhaps some will.

I've led workshops in rooms that have a fireplace. That is not a welcome addition on a July afternoon in Iowa, but during much of the year, arranging your sessions around a fireplace is lovely. Some buildings have large windows that look out unto beautiful trees or rugged mountains or even a collection of bird feeders. Arranging the seating so that people can enjoy that view enhances your event.

If you are serving a meal, offer something different than what your guests have for lunch at the office every day. You may not be able to manage a home-cooked meal, but perhaps one thing, the soup or the bread or the dessert, can be homemade. If that is not possible, even a small luxury serves well: some fruit chutney to put on the meat, fresh berries in the salad, honey butter or cinnamon butter for the bread. Can you use real dishes instead of plastic? How about bright cloth napkins instead of paper ones? If you have the resources, you might invite each guest to keep their own cloth napkin as a gift.

If your guests sit at tables for the sessions, you could put a chocolate kiss or a wrapped piece of dark chocolate at each place, like the luxury hotels that welcome you to your room with a small chocolate mint on your pillow. If you do that, have a dish of sugar-free candy available for those who prefer it.

I provide each guest with a folder to hold information, handouts, and announcements of future retreats. I use the bright colored two pocket folders. In August when school supplies fill store shelves, they are often on sale for a few cents apiece, and I stock up then. I like to add something to the folder that is just for fun (like a page of pencil or word games) or that is inspiring (a printed card with a prayer, a quote or a beautiful photo.)

You can think of other ways to make participants feel welcome. In a culture where everyone has way too much to do, these people have given up other opportunities and precious time to join you. These small gestures of kindness are your way of saying thank you. They give the message that the day will be full of good things, and your guests will begin the work with an open spirit.

THE COMMUNITY

Will everyone know each other? Will most folks know one another, but a few will not, and thus there is a risk of their feeling ill at ease, or left out? Or will most people be strangers to one another? That will determine how you shape this event, especially in the opening session.

Use nametags. A sign might instruct people to write their first name only; that makes it easier for people to learn each other's names. If they print their name in big, dark letters (use dark markers instead of pens), folks can see it from a distance, which allows people to use each other's name. Or you may prefer to have names tags made ahead of time that give the participants' full name and the city or faith community or organization from which they come. If folks are seated around tables, it can be helpful to fold a large index card in half, print their name in large letters on one half, and set it in front of participant, facing the others in the room.

If the building is unfamiliar to any participants, let them know where they can find bathrooms, elevators, and meals.

It is wise to begin the first session (and each session or each day, if you have time) with opportunities to get acquainted, and to relax, laugh, move, and loosen up. What you choose will depend on how well participants already know each other, and how many people are in the group. You may have some favorite ice-breakers or community building games, and there are books that offer many others. Here are a few that I've found effective.

- Leader begins with a sentence that starts with A: "A funny thing happened on my way to this gathering…." The next person must continue the story with a sentence that begins with B. Continue through the group and the alphabet. This can lead to a lot of laughter.

- Each person tells his or her first (or middle) name and briefly mentions any story about that name. Why did your parents choose it? Do you like it?

- On participant's forehead or back, attach the name of a famous person. They might be people in history, in your faith tradition, holy people or saints, biblical characters, or in keeping with this workshop, people known for their work for peace. Everyone mills around asking questions to try to guess who they are, according to the sign they are wearing but cannot see. They may ask only yes or no questions, and only one question per person before they move on to ask someone else.

- Each person names three things about themselves that people would not know. Two of those things are true, one is not. The group tries to guess which one is not.

- Depending on the season, each person in turn gives his or her name and tells the best Christmas gift they ever received, or the funniest birthday gift, or the best valentine, etc.

- Each person gives his or her name and favorite food (or book, film, sport, etc.)

- Each person gives their name and their favorite toy when they were about ten.

- The first person says her first name. The next repeats her name, and adds his own. It continues this way until the last person is having to repeat all the names before adding his or her own.

- Each person says his first name and couples it with an adjective describing himself or herself: Gorgeous George, Silly Susan, etc.

- Put just enough seats in a circle for everyone but you (musical chairs style). You stand in the center and say, "The Big Wind blows on everyone who…" and then add your own description: is wearing white socks; has gotten a speeding ticket; likes Brussels sprouts, has a dog…. Everyone who fits the description must get up and change seats, and you try to get one, also. Whoever is left without a seat gets to be the Big Wind. If the Big Wind yells "hurricane" then everyone has to change seats.

- People Scavenger Hunt. Each participant is given a sheet of paper with experiences. People mill around hunting for someone who has had one of the experiences, who will then initial that line. Depending on the size of the group, you will need to set a limit: each person may initial anyone's list only once (or only twice) even if they qualify for more. The experiences on the sheet should be tailored to this group, and some should be humorous. You will want ten to twenty experiences. Here's some examples:

- ▪ I am fluent in at least two languages._____
- ▪ I have fallen asleep during a sermon._____
- ▪ I have received a traffic ticket in the past year._____
- ▪ I tweet._____
- ▪ I love rutabagas. _____
- ▪ I am wearing something purple today. _____
- ▪ I check Facebook every day._____
- ▪ I have a hole in my sock today. _____

- Name someone you would like to have lunch and conversation with. This person may be living or dead. Why did you choose this person?

- Name the fictional character—from book or film—that you would most like to meet and hang out with for awhile. Why did you choose this character?

SAMPLE RETREAT SCHEDULES

Here are some suggestions to help you plan your retreat or workshop. I have offered different options: a one-day workshop, an overnight or weekend retreat and a series of weekly classes. You will not be able to use all the material in the book; you will have to choose. The times are not meant to be rigid; you might to spend more time, perhaps, on those areas that stimulate a lot of energetic discussion. You will also need to decide if you want to offer an intense retreat with lots of content and minimal free time, or if you want to shorten the content and offer a more contemplative, restorative event with extended free time. The following schedules do not allow 5 or 10 minutes between sessions but you will want to include such cushions in your planning. Between a community building activity and the next session, for example, people may make quick stops in the bathroom, or use their cell phones. If the group must move to a different area or building, you will certainly have to adjust the times to allow for that....and expect the transition to be slower than you think it will be!

If these schedules feel too crowded and rushed, you can work with only two of the "*bless them*" options and only two of the "*change me*" options. This book offers three options for each, making six areas of focus. You can choose the ones you want, and work with only four focus areas.

OUTLINE FOR AN OVERNIGHT RETREAT

Evening:

4:00—5:00	People gather, settle into their rooms
5:15	Welcome. Supper.
	or:
	omit supper, arriving and settling in between 5:00 and 6:00
6:00	Welcome, housekeeping (Where are the bathrooms? What are the rules or expectations of our hosts? etc.) Ice-breakers; community building activities (See page 89-91)
7:00	A time for worship, meditation, chanting or singing
7:20	First session: use the material in Chapter 1.
9:00 or 9:30	Closing prayer or blessing

Following Day

7:00-8:00	Breakfast
8:00	A time of worship, meditation, chanting or singing
8:15-11:30	Session using material in Chapters 2, 3, 4: three ways to bless them. Schedule a break of at least 15 minutes in the midst of this session. If you finish before 11:30, move on to Chapter 5 or give the group a longer break for lunch and free time.
11:30-1:00	Lunch and free time
1:00-4:00	Session using material in Chapters 5,6,7,8: three ways to change me. Offer at least a 15-minute break in the midst of this session.
4:00	Feedback, evaluations, closing worship or blessing
4:30	Retreat ends

OUTLINE FOR A WEEKEND RETREAT

If you have the luxury of a full weekend for your retreat, you can have more in- depth discussions and activities and also offer a slower, more contemplative experience. Here is a possible schedule if you begin on Friday evening.

Friday Evening

4:00—5:00	People gather, settle into their rooms
5:15	Welcome. Supper.
	or:
	omit supper, arriving and settling in between 5:00 and 6:00
6:00	Welcome, housekeeping (Where are the bathrooms? What are the rules or expectations of our hosts? etc.) Ice-breakers; community building activities (See page 89-91)
7:00	A time for worship, meditation, chanting or singing
7:20	First session: use the material in Chapter 1.
9:00 or 9:30	Closing prayer or blessing

Saturday Morning

7:00-8:00	Breakfast
8:00-8:30	Free time, but encourage people to use this time for personal devotions, for walking outside, or for sitting in silence.
8:30-9:00	A time of worship, chanting, or singing, and perhaps another activity to help people get acquainted and to pull the group together.
9:00-noon	Use the material from Chapters 2 and 3, including many opportunities to share with others, to do some of the activities, to write in a journal.

	Plan a 20-minute break during the morning.
noon-2:00	Lunch and free time
2:00-4:00	Return to anything that did not get finished in the morning. Be sure to ask if people have any questions, confusion or concerns. (Ask that often throughout the retreat.) Then work with the material from Chapter 4. Include at least a 15-minute break here.
5:00-7:00	Supper and free time
7:00-8:00	At this point you have completed the "Bless them" half of the material. It is a good time to summarize the three "Bless them" suggestions. Perhaps you can ask participants to name other "Bless them" ideas that we could have included.
8:00	You have options here: end the day with a brief worship. Prayer or singing; offer free time; or plan a concert, dance, or film.

Sunday

7:00	Breakfast
8:00-9:00	If your group is used to Sunday morning worship, offer that. If not, you can move right into the sessions, or leave this hour as free time, or encourage people to use it for personal meditation or for walking outside.
9:00-noon	Use the material in Chapters 5 and 6. Remember to plan a break.
noon-1:30	Lunch and free time
1:30-3:00	Use the material in Chapters 7 and 8.
3:00-4:00	Closure: evaluations and feedback, worship, opportunity to make a commitment (See page 121)
4:00	Retreat ends.

OUTLINE FOR A ONE DAY (6 HOURS) WORKSHOP

9:30	Gathering; coffee/tea
10:00	Welcome, introductions, hymn, chant or prayer
10:15-12:15	Session using material in Chapters 1,2,3,4 Offer at least a 15- minute break midway through this session.
12:15-1:00	Lunch
1:00-3:30	Session using material in Chapters 5,6,7,8 Offer at least a 15- minute break midway through this session.
3:30-4:00	Feedback, evaluations, closing worship or blessing, opportunity to make a commitment (See "Commitment" on page 121)
4:00	Workshop ends

SUGGESTIONS FOR WEEKLY CLASSES

If you choose to meet weekly, you must decide on the length of each session. One hour does not allow much time to get into good discussions, though you can make that work if you need to, especially if you can schedule more sessions. A two-hour class taxes people's endurance, though that allows for plenty of time to work in depth, and you can schedule a break in the middle. A session lasting one and one-half hours is often a good choice.

If you schedule a class for 8 weeks, you can plan to focus on one chapter of this book each week. If you are planning 6 weeks, you will need to combine chapters a bit.

If you have only 4 or 5 weeks, you can choose just two of the "*Bless them*" issues and just two of the "*Change me*" issues so as to have plenty of time for discussion and for Chapter 8.

In making a choice between more content or more interaction, choose more interaction. It is more valuable for people to share with one another or participate in discussions than for the class to cover everything that would be great to include.

Although your time is limited if you are doing weekly sessions, it is still important to have introductions and a moment of silence, a prayer, or a short song or inspirational reading to set the tone of the gathering, and to help the group settle in together.

SUGGESTIONS FOR WORSHIP, REFLECTION OR MEDITATION

I recommend that your workshop begin and end with a time of worship, silence, chanting or reflection. This will center your group and re-enforce the values you are promoting through this material.

This time can be very simple: a song or chant, a prayer or reading, some silence, another song or chant and words of blessing. If you want to, you can include more readings, a guided meditation, or a ritual that is meaningful in your tradition. You might want to include an invitation for participants to make a commitment to this work. On page 121, I will offer a way to do that.

Though you will have prayers or readings that are meaningful to your group, I am including some others that you might use. Adapt them to fit your community, using faith language or not as you need. If your retreat is done in the context of a faith tradition, you can address prayers to God or Spirit or Holy One or any of the endless ways to name the Source of all. If your group is secular, you can still offer prayer, but without addressing it to an "Other." If your group is squeamish about reading from a particular scripture, (the Bible, for instance), they will usually appreciate that reading if you include readings from other world wisdom traditions as well.

If you print any of the following readings, be sure to add the appropriate credit.

Reading from the Christian scripture:

But I say to you that listen, Love your enemies,
do good to those who hate you, bless those who
curse you, pray for those who abuse you. If any-
one strikes you on the cheek, offer the other also,
and from anyone who take away your coat do
not withhold even your shirt. Give to everyone
who begs from you, and if anyone takes away
your goods, do not ask for them again. Do to
others as you would have them do to you. ...
Do not judge and you will not be judged; do not
condemn and you will not be condemned. For-
give and your will be forgiven; give and it will
be given back to you. A good measure, pressed
down, shaken together, running over, will be put
into your lap; for the measure you give will be
the measure you get back.
(Luke 6:27-31, 37-38)

I, therefore, the prisoner in the Lord, beg you
to lead a life worthy of the calling to which you
have been called, with all humility and gentle-
ness, with patience, bearing with one another in
love, making every effort to maintain the unity
of the Spirit in the bond of peace.
(Ephesians 4:1-3)

Reading from the Buddhist scripture, The Dhammapada, Chapter 1, verses 1-5

Our life is shaped by our mind; we become what we think. Suffering follows an evil thought as the wheels of a cart follow the oxen that draw it.

Our life is shaped by our mind; we become what we think. Joy follows a pure thought like a shadow that never leaves.

"He was angry with me, he attacked me, he defeated me, he robbed me"—those who dwell on such thoughts will never be free from hatred.

"He was angry with me, he attacked me, he defeated me, he robbed me"—those who do not dwell on such thoughts will surely become free from hatred.

For hatred can never put an end to hatred. love alone can. This is an unalterable law.

(The Twin Verses. Translated by Eknath Easwaran The Dhammapada. The Nilgiri Press:Tomales, CA. 1985. page 78)

READING FROM THE HINDU SCRIPTURE, THE RIG VEDA:

May we be united in heart.
May we be united in speech.
May we be united in mind.
May we perform our duties as did the wise of old.
May we be united in our prayer.
May we be united in our goal.
May we be united in our resolve.
May we be united in our understanding.
May we be united in our offering.
May we be united in our feelings.
May we be united in our hearts.
May we be united in our thoughts.
May there be perfect unity among us.

(Translated by Eknath Easwaran. Timeless Wisdom. Nilgiri Press: Tomales, CA. 2008. page 13)

READING FROM CHINESE SCRIPTURE, THE TAO TE CHING (#31)

Weapons are tools of violence;
all decent men detest them.
Weapons are tools of fear;
a decent man will avoid them
except in the direst necessity
and, if compelled, will use them
only with the utmost restraint.
Peace is his highest value.
If the peace has been shattered,
how can he be content?
His enemies are not demons,
but human beings like himself.

He doesn't wish them personal harm.
Nor does he rejoice in victory.
How could he rejoice in victory
and delight in the slaughter of men?

He enters a battle gravely,
with sorrow and great compassion,
as if he were attending a funeral.

(Translated by Stephen Mitchell. Tao Te Ching.
Harper & Row: New York. 1988)

READING FROM JEWISH SCRIPTURE

When a stranger sojourns with you in your land,
you shall not do him wrong. The stranger who
sojourns with you shall be to you as the native
among you, and you shall love him as yourself;
for you were strangers in the land of Egypt: I am
the Lord your God.   (Leviticus 19:33-34)

If you meet your enemy's ox or his ass gone astray,
you shall bring it back to him. If you see the ass
of one who hates you lying under its burden, you
shall refrain from leaving him with it, you shall
help him to lift it up. (Exodus 23:4-5)

If your enemy is hungry, give him bread to eat,
and if he is thirsty, give him water to drink.
(Proverbs 25:21)

I hate, I despise your feasts, and I take no delight
in your solemn assemblies. Even though you offer
me your burnt offers and cereal offerings, I will
not accept them, and the peace offerings of your
fatted beasts I will not look upon. Take away

*from me the noise of your songs; to the melody of
your harps I will not listen. But let justice roll
down like waters and righteousness like an ev-
er-flowing stream
(Amos 5:21-24)*

READING FROM ISLAMIC SCRIPTURE: THE QUR'AN (TRANSLATED BY THOMAS CLEARY)

*Worship nothing but God;
be good to your parents and relatives,
and to the orphan and the poor.
Speak nicely to people,
be constant in prayer,
and give charity. (The Cow, 83)*

*Serve God
and do not associate
anything with God.
And be good to your parents
and relative
and to orphans and paupers
and to neighbors close by
and neighbors remote,
and to the companion at your side,
and to the traveler,
and to your wards.*

(Women. 36)

PRAYERS

Holy One,
Sometimes we feel like this;
I don't want to talk to them.
I can't get along with them.
I am against them and they're against me.
Their opinions make me sore.
What they stand for I deplore.
I just want to turn away and go out the door.

But it is in the presence of these very people
that you call us to the table,
the table we share with them.

We want to be peacemakers.
Grant us courage.
We want to love.
Fill us with the power of Jesus, so we can.
And give us the capacity to pray this prayer:
Bless them. Change me. Amen.
(© Janice Jean Springer 2006)

When it seemed there was no peace, O Lord,
you showed us new ways to peace.
When it seemed there was too much hate, O Lord,
you showed us new ways to love.
When it seemed there were only endings,
you showed us new beginnings.
Strengthen our belief in the power of life over death.
Strengthen our trust in the power of love over hate,
that we may be bearers of peace in the world, O Lord,
that we may be bearers of peace.
(adapted from J. Philip Newell. Celtic Treasure.
Grand Rapids, MI; Erdmans, 2005. p. 106.)

Loving Kindness (Metta) Meditation

> *May I be happy.*
> *May I be peaceful.*
> *May I be free.*

> *May my friends be happy.*
> *May my friends be peaceful.*
> *May my friends be free.*

> *May my enemies be happy.*
> *May my enemies be peaceful.*
> *May my enemies be free.*

> *May all beings be happy.*
> *May all beings be peaceful.*
> *May all beings be free.*

(You can substitute other qualities for the words happy, peaceful, free, such as safe, healthy, loved. Be cautious, though, about turning this blessing into a veiled accusation or obligation, using words like kind, patient, forgiving. This blessing is a gift, not a judgment or a spiritual to-do list.)

Creator God,
You call us to welcome friend and stranger.
You call us to offer safety and shelter.
You call us to make room.
Yet, our lives are already so crowded.

Today, we make room for you,
and invite you to clear our inner spaces
so we will be able to make room
for whomever you send to us. Amen.
(© Janice Jean Springer 2016)

Holy Mystery, you call us to love:
love you, love neighbor, love self, love enemy.
But it is very hard.
If we are to answer your call to love,
we need community to sustain us,
Spirit to empower us,
and you to immerse us in grace.

God of Many Names, you call us to care,
to care for those in need,
to care for friend, stranger, enemy.
But it is very hard.
If we are to answer your call to care,
we need community to sustain us,
Spirit to empower us,
and you to immerse us in grace.
May it be so.
(© Janice Jean Springer 2016)

O God, enlarge our hearts,
that they may be big enough to receive your love.
Stretch our hearts
that they may have room for all those you love,
all those who are not lovely in our eyes,

> *all those whose hands we don't want to touch,*
> *but who depend on us to be your body.*
> *Heal our hearts,*
> *so that we might have the courage*
> *and the capacity to love. Amen.*
> *(adapted from an African prayer in Prayer En-*
> *circling the World; Westminster. p.108)*

OPTIONAL ACTIVITIES IF NEEDED

It is a good idea to prepare more material than you expect to need, just in case. Here are some additional activities that you might have in your back pocket. And it may be that an activity suggested at the end of a chapter of this book does not quite work for your group. If so, you can use one of these instead.

Activity A:

One author offers a wonderful, rather uncomfortable exercise on enemy imaging in everyday life. Let's try part of it.

1. Think of someone with whom you are in conflict, or whom you just dislike. This could be a boss, a coworker, a relative, an ex-spouse, a church member, the president.

2. How do you feel when you think about this person?

3. How much energy do you invest in putting this person down? How does this affect you?

4. How much do you enjoy getting agreement with your allies about how bad s/he is?

5. How much do you avoid or limit communication with this person?

6. To what extent does putting this person down make you feel good about yourself? How aware are you of all the ways in which you are better than him/her?

7. How uncomfortable do you feel if you get information about this person that contradicts your theory about him/her?

8. How reluctant are you to change your opinion and let go of your dislike? What would you be giving up?

(Diane Perlman. "From Changing the Image of the Enemy." Reprinted in *Peacemaking Without Division.* Patricia Washburn and Robert Gribbon. p.33.)

• •

Activity B:

I have chosen three ways we could *bless them* and three ways we could *change me*.

Invite participants to think of three (or one or two) different ways to *bless them*, and three (or one or two) different ways to *change me*. If time permits, you can ask them to briefly name how we might live out their new prayers for blessing and changing. For example, if I were doing this for the material in Chapter 4, it might look like this:

- Cherish their story.
    - ☒ listen without judging
    - ☒ listen without interrupting with my story
    - ☒ listen without giving advice
    - ☒ listen with an open heart

This exercise can be done by individuals or pairs, but it especially lends itself to a small group working together.

• •

Activity C:

If you want to cherish another person's story, here are some conversation guidelines.

- Open-mindedness: Listen to and respect all points of view.
- Acceptance: Suspend judgment as best you can.
- Curiosity: Seek to understand rather than persuade.
- Discovery: Question assumptions; look for new insights.
- Sincerity: Speak what has personal meaning for you.
- Brevity: Go for honesty and depth, but don't go on and on.

1. Invite each person to pick one of these and share with another or a small group a time when someone practiced that guideline when listening to you. How did that feel? What effect did it have on your sharing?

2. In a small group, share which one of these guidelines is the easiest for you to do. Which one is the hardest for you? What helps you be able to practice that guideline, at least a little?

    (from *Yes!* magazine, Winter 2008 p.25. Vicki Robin)

• •

Activity D:

Give each person a card with these words: *Sometimes I perceive as an enemy those people who....* Each one finishes the sentence, for example:

- are pro-choice

- patronize women

- are lesbian or gay

- are fundamentalist Christians

- are from the middle-East, especially Muslims

- make racist comments

After each one has finished their sentence, each person in turn reads their sentence aloud, recognizing that it takes a bit of courage to do that since someone in the group might be in a category named as an enemy. The group will listen respectfully without comment.

• •

Activity E:

Great spiritual teachers say that we need our enemies; they always have gifts for us. Make a list of people (or situations, institutions, qualities in yourself) whom you might name as enemy: someone who has hurt you, someone with whom you disagree, someone who stands in the way of something you want, some part of yourself that you don't like, some group that didn't accept you, etc. No one will see this list. Then write a word or a sentence naming any gift that enemy gave you. Examples:

- Martha…I saw how much I always want to be right

- depression…After much struggle, I learned to give voice, to speak up.

- my doctor…. I learned to trust my inner wisdom, to listen to my intuition.

Without naming a specific person or institution, choose one on your list and share the gift you received from that one.

• •

Activity F:

Read this poem, and invite people to respond to these questions:

- When were you able to see Christ in the face of someone you met? What was that like?

- Can you think of a time when you failed to see Christ in the face of another? What was that like?

The Vase
I pray for
the grace
to sit at
the feet
of each
person I meet
and see Christ
in their face.

(Kent Ira Groff,
*Active Spirituality:
a Guide for Seekers and Ministers.*
Alban Institute, 1993, p.138.)

• •

HANDOUTS

You have permission to copy the handouts offered here for use with the material in this book. If there is a credit on the bottom of the page, you must include that credit. You may also add the date and sponsor of your workshop, if you wish.

The first handout is a summary of the workshop. I suggest you give it to participants at the end of your time together.

The second handout is a list of resources for further study. Feel free to add more ideas to this list.

Each handout is printed here on a separate page, copy ready.

You can find links to download copy-ready 8 1/2" x 11" copies of these handouts at https://welcomeat-thetable.site.

O God, bless them. Change me.

Bless them:
Pray for their well-being.
not for their conversion to my perspective
Be willing to feel at least a little of their pain.
lower my defenses: staying in my intellect, being very busy, problem solving, etc.

relate out of my heart as well as my head

be fully, totally present to them and their story
Cherish their story.
listen without judging or "setting them right"

listen without jumping in with my story

listen without problem-solving or giving advice

listen without planning what I want to say as soon as it's my turn

listen with an open heart

<u>**Change me:**</u>
Be willing to be vulnerable.
>state my feelings instead of my opinions/thoughts
>listen without defending my idea
>let go of defenses such as arrogance, self-righ-teousness
>share my pain without blaming

Refuse to diminish another person.
>stereotyping, labeling
>dismissing their ideas
>perceiving them as one-dimensional
>feeling superior to them
>assuming they are wrong

Talk from my feelings instead of my thoughts.
>ideas, opinions, and thoughts invite conflict
>experiences and feelings invite compassion

© 2005 Janice Jean Springer
janice@welcomeatthetable.site

A FEW GOOD RESOURCES....

Bechtle, Mike. *People Can't Drive You Crazy if You Don't Give Them the Keys.* ISBN#: 978-0800721114. Revell. 2012.

How to stop being a victim of other people's craziness.

Beck, Richard. *Stranger God: Meeting Jesus in Disguise.* (Minneapolis: Fortress Press, 2017).

Beck, Richard. *Unclean: Meditations on Purity, Hospitality and Mortality.* (Eugene, OR: Cascade Books, 2011).

Berry, Wendell. *Blessed are the Peacemakers.* ISBN#: 978-1593761004. (Shoemaker Hoard, 2005).

A short book of Jesus' teachings on peace and two essays in response.

Chopra, Deepak. *Peace is the Way.* ISBN#: 978-0307339812. (Harmony, 2005).

Drawing on Hindu tradition, modern medicine and psychology.

Haidt, Jonathan. *The Righteous Mind.*

Why good people are divided by politics and religion.

Hahn, Thich Nhat. *Creating True Peace.* ISBN#: 978-0743245203. (Atria Reprinted edition, 2004).

Universal ideas about living in peace with one another.

Kasl, Charlotte. *if the Buddha were married.* ISBN#: 978-0140196221. (Penguin Books, 2001).

From Buddhist, Sufi, Quaker: how to live in committed relationships

Law. Eric H. F. *The Wolf Shall Dwell with the Lamb.* ISBN#: 978-0827242319. (Chalice Press. 1993).

Dealing with culture clashes in multicultural communities.

Lozoff, Bo. *It's a Meaningful Life.* ISBN#: 978-0140196245. (Penguin Compass, 2001).

Spiritual practices that foster peace, community, respect.

Rohr, Richard. *The Naked Now.* ISBN#: 978-0824525439. The (Crossroad Publishing Company. 2009).

The inner transformation needed if we are to transform the world.

Rosenberg, Marshall B. *Nonviolent Communication.* ISBN#: 978-1892005281. (Puddledancer Press. 2015).

How to talk in ways that foster peace and respect.

Rosenberg, Marshall B. *Speak Peace in a World of Conflict.* ISBN#: 978-1892005175. (Puddledancer Press. 2005).

How to talk in ways that foster peace and respect.

Tutu, Desmond and Mpho Tutu. *The Book of Forgiving.* ISBN#: 978-0062203571. (HarperOne. 2015).

Forgiveness as the path to healing community.

Vanier, Jean. *From Brokenness to Community.* ISBN#: 978-0809133413. (Paulist Press. 1992).

Helping us love those who are difficult, those we name enemy.

Vennard, Jane E. *Praying for Friends and Enemies.* ISBN#: 978-0806627694. (Augsburg Fortress. 1992).

How to pray for others, especially when it is hard to do.

Also look at other titles by these authors.

GOOD WEB SITES

cacradicalgrace.org (Center for Action and Contemplation; Richard Rohr)

humankindness.org (Human Kindness Foundation promoting spiritual life and service) tikkun.org (Jewish origin; interfaith movement; for repair and transformation of world)

cnvc.org (Center for Non-violent Communication; Marshall Rosenberg)

peacemaker.net (Peacemaker Ministries helps Christians learn to handle conflict)

fetzer.org (Foundation that helps to build the spiritual foundation for a loving world)

afsc.org (Quaker organization promoting peace with justice as expression of faith in action)

theforgivenessproject.com (Secular organization promoting forgiveness and healing)

COMMITMENT

When, near the end of your gathering, you have passed out the summary of the retreat— three ways we could bless our enemy and three ways we could change ourselves—invite people to take a moment to review it. In pairs or small groups, ask participants to share which of the six options would be the hardest for them to do.

It is easy for us to hear these ideas and then go home and never think of them again. After all, life moves on—and at high speed. So, as the sessions come near to the end, invite people to take an index card and choose one—only one; any one—of the six possibilities which they will commit to work on for one month. Ask them to write their choice on the card, and share with someone in the group which one they have chosen. Invite them to take the card home and put it where they will see it every day—on the bathroom mirror, on the refrigerator, on their screen saver--so they can remember this one-month commitment.

Learning a new skill and practicing a new discipline is most likely to be successful if we have a buddy to support us. Suggest to the group that they choose someone from the group—even someone they don't know very well—and agree to check in with each other, perhaps once a week, to encourage each other and have a safe place to talk about how their effort is going. Or they could choose a friend or family member who is willing to offer that support, even if they have not taken the class.

In your closing worship or ritual, you can bless these commitments and those trying to practice them.

WHAT TO BRING TO THE WORKSHOP, RETREAT OR CLASSES

Here are things you will need for the workshop, retreat or classes. Adapt this list to your situation and then use it as a checklist when you are gathering resources for this event.

• pens and paper for each person (unless you have asked people to bring their own)

• a nurturing focal point: fabric, live plant or flowers, candle, symbol of spiritual tradition, rocks or shells, etc. This can be on a table in some central place and/or you can put a mini-version of this on each table.

• handouts:

1.   summary of the six options
2.   list of resources: books and websites
3.   page of quotes related to this topic

• posters with quotes hanging around the room
• name tags and dark markers
• songbooks or song sheets if needed
• drinks and snacks
• meal provisions if needed
• books for display
• blank index cards, one for each person and a few extra
• perhaps water glasses and water pitcher at each table
• any supplies needed for community building activities (for instance, copies of People's Scavenger Hunt)

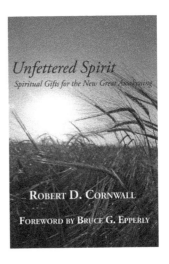

MORE FROM ENERGION PUBLICATIONS

ACADEMY OF PARISH CLERGY SERIES AND AUTHORS

Conversations in Ministry

Clergy Table Talk	Kent Ira Groff	$9.99
Out of the Office	Robert D. Cornwall	$9.99
Wind and Whirlwind	David Moffett-Moore	$9.99

Guides to Practical Ministry

Overcoming Sermon Block	William Powell Tuck	$12.99
Thrive	Ruth Fletcher	$14.99
In Changing Times	Ron Higdon	$14.99

Academy Member Authors (Selected Titles)

Faith in the Public Square	Robert D. Cornwall	$16.99
Ephesians: A Participatory Study Guide		$9.99
Ultimate Allegiance		$9.99
The Authority of Scripture in a Postmodern Age		$5.99
From Words of Woe to Unbelievable News		$5.99
The Eucharist		$5.99
Unfettered Spirit		$14.99
From Here to Eternity	Bruce Epperly	$5.99
Angels, Mysteries, and Miracles		$9.99
Transforming Acts		$14.99
Jonah: When God Changes		$5.99
Process Theology: Embracing Adventure with God		$5.99
The Journey to the Undiscovered Country	William Powell Tuck	$9.99
Lord, I Keep Getting a Busy Signal		$9.99
The Last Words from the Cross		$9.99
The Church Under the Cross		$9.99
Creation in Contemporary Experience	David Moffett-Moore	$9.99
Life as Pilgrimage		$14.99
The Spirit's Fruit		$9.99
The Jesus Manifesto		$9.99
Spiritual Care Reflections	Charles J. Lopez, Jr.	$14.99
Surviving a Son's Suicide	Ron Higdon	$9.99
All I Need to Know I'm Still Learning at 80		

Generous Quantity Discounts Available
Dealer Inquiries Welcome
Energion Publications — P.O. Box 841
Gonzalez, FL_ 32560
Website: http://energionpubs.com
Phone: (850) 525-3916